SCOTLAND'S
TRUE HERITAGE PUBS

Pub Interiors of Special Historic Interest

Edited by **Michael Slaughter**

**CAMPAIGN
FOR
REAL ALE**

Produced by CAMRA's Pub Heritage Group,
with support from CAMRA Books; Debbie Williams and Helen Ridge.

Published by the Campaign for Real Ale Ltd,
230 Hatfield Road, St Albans, Hertfordshire AL1 4LW
tel: 01727 867201   fax: 01727 867670
e-mail: camra@camra.org.uk
website: www.camra.org.uk

Design/typography: Dale Tomlinson
Map: John Macklin
Printed in the United Kingdom by Stones the Printers, Banbury, Oxon

ISBN 13: 978-1-85249-242-7

Photographs © Michael Slaughter, apart from those of the
Fiddichside Inn, Craigellachie, which are by George Howie.
The historic photograph of the Douglas Arms Hotel, Banchory,
is reproduced by kind permission of Banchory Historical Society.
CAMRA is grateful to Rudolph Kenna and Anthony Mooney
for allowing it to reproduce plans from their classic book
People's Palaces: Victorian and Edwardian Pubs of Scotland (1983).

This guide is a result of the work carried out over a number of years
by Stuart Wallace who suggested candidates for inclusion and,
together with Ken Davie, George Howie and Colin Valentine,
formed the steering group. Grateful thanks go to the members
of the Scottish branches of CAMRA who have suggested pubs,
and to Ian Whyte for his knowledge of historic pubs in Edinburgh.

Editor's Acknowledgements
I am very grateful to Geoff Brandwood for his numerous suggestions,
improvements and corrections; and to David Lawrence and
George Williamson for their helpful advice and proofreading.

Front cover photo: first floor bar at Café Royal, Edinburgh.
Back cover photo: Bennet's Bar, Edinburgh.
Inside back cover photo: Old Toll Bar, Glasgow.

Contents

Introduction

A Celebration of Scottish Pub Heritage

Scotland's True Heritage Pubs is a guide to a splendidly varied collection of pubs with the best and most interesting interiors in the whole of Scotland. It is CAMRA's pioneering initiative to bring greater appreciation of the most valuable historic pub interiors in the country to both local people and tourists. Although Scotland has over 4,000 public houses, this guide lists just 115. There are so few because of the enormous amount of opening out, theming and general modernisation that has taken place in recent decades. Safeguarding what is now left of the country's pub heritage has become a serious conservation challenge. By publishing this guide, we aim to encourage owners and local authorities to take steps to ensure these establishments remain genuine historic pubs for years to come.

This guide develops work started by CAMRA in the early 1990s to identify those pubs in the United Kingdom that still retained their historic interiors more or less intact. The work resulted in the *National Inventory of Pub Interiors of Outstanding Historic Interest*, an up-to-date edition of which is printed in the annual *Good Beer Guide*. Out of a total of 254 pubs listed in the current inventory, 32 are in Scotland (identified in this guide by ★). The pubs in this guide are very largely as they were before the mid-1960s (when the orgy of pub refitting and opening out began) or, if they have been expanded, this has been done sensitively and without destroying the historic heart. The survival of multiple rooms and old furnishings and fittings has been crucial to the selection. More information about the CAMRA project to save the nation's genuine historic pubs appears on page 13.

Characteristics of Scottish Pubs

Tenements

One of the most distinctive exterior features of thousands of Scottish pubs and also the most noticeable difference between them and pubs in other parts of the UK is that they occupy the ground floors of tenement blocks of flats alongside a variety of shops. Tenements are Scotland's dominant style of urban house building in the European tradition, compared to England, Wales and Ireland where the main style is the terraced house. This means that many Scottish pubs are

Left: The island serving counter and gantry with ticket-booth type windows and original Bryson clock at Leslie's Bar, Edinburgh.

Leslie's Bar in the Newington area of Edinburgh is built at the foot of a four-storey tenement building.

often little different from adjacent shop-fronts, while pubs in other parts of the UK tend to be the only building on the plot, whether freestanding or part of a terrace. In Scotland, most pubs do not have living accommodation for licensees, due to early 20th-century legislation that made Sunday opening illegal. As a result, pubs were known as 'lock-ups'.

Island Serving Counters

Up until the 1880s, pubs in Scottish towns and cities had small bar rooms and a number of other sitting rooms, similar to pubs in other parts of the UK. In their classic book *People's Palaces* about the pubs of Scotland in the Victorian and Edwardian era, Rudolph Kenna and Anthony Mooney state that these old-time pubs were proving unacceptable to the licensing magistrates of Glasgow and other Scottish towns and cities, who claimed that the publican and his assistants were unable to exercise overall supervision over their customers. From 1885 to the early 1900s, many of these pubs were consequently remodelled to create a spacious and often lofty room with a large island serving counter, usually oval in shape but sometimes circular, elongated oval, square or even octagonal, and an ornately carved central fitment holding mainly casks of whisky and occasionally other spirits. Most pubs were designed for stand-up drinking, but some sitting rooms, as they are known, were provided, usually at the front of the pub, and well lit to meet the approval of the authorities.

The plans below show the layout of the Blane Valley (Change House) in Glasgow before and after alterations in 1887. Here, a U-shaped bar counter has been chosen. More common was the island bar situated in the centre of the room as the plan of MacSorley's, Glasgow shows. Note there is a separate luncheon bar (one still exists at the Abbotsford, Edinburgh) but no sitting rooms and a limited amount of seating – stand-up drinking was the norm.

The first two plans are of the Blane Valley (Change House) in Glasgow. The third plan is of MacSorley's, also Glasgow.

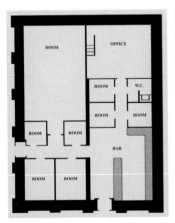

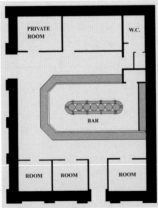

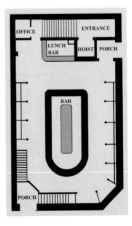

The island serving counters here at the Abbotsford and also at Leslie's Bar, both in Edinburgh, are unusual in that there is no central fitment to house the spirits, glasses etc. Instead, there is a sturdy wooden superstructure on top of the counter.

There are a number of pubs with island serving counters featured in this guide, the finest being the Horseshoe Bar, Glasgow, where the counter is an elongated horseshoe shape some 32 metres (104 feet) in circumference. According to the *Guinness Book of Records*, it is the longest pub bar counter in the whole of the UK. The Railway Tavern, Shettleston, on the east side of Glasgow, is the most intact of the island bar style of pub: it has retained two sitting rooms and, even more remarkably, an intact family department (off-sales).

Other pubs with central counters of significance from late Victorian and Edwardian times are Pittodrie Bar, Aberdeen; Kenilworth, Edinburgh; and Phoenix, Inverness. A popular variation of the island style is the U-shaped serving counter protruding from a wall, as seen at Market Inn, Ayr, and Central Bar, Renton.

Later examples of note can be seen at Prestoungrange Gothenburg, Prestonpans; examples from the 1930s are at Lang's Bar, Paisley, and Portland Arms, Shettleston. At the Railway, West Calder, and the Woodside, Falkirk, the area for the staff is about the same size as the U-shaped area around the bar for drinkers. The huge island serving counters in Fanny by Gaslight, Kilmarnock; Town Arms, Selkirk and Prince of Wales, Port Glasgow, have been shortened in recent times to increase the drinking space.

Ornate Gantries with Spirit Casks

From the 1890s, a number of pubs were refitted with a straight bar counter and an ornately carved fitting behind, holding polished spirit casks and decorated with mirrored centrepieces, often advertising brewery or distillery products. This fitting is known as a 'gantry', derived from 'gantress', or 'gauntress', an old Scots words to describe a wooden stand for casks, which you can find mounted both vertically and on their sides. A number of examples of gantries can also be found in Ireland, which, like Scotland, has a long history of spirit drinking.

The finest example of this style of pub is the Old Toll Bar, Glasgow, which has ornate mirrors extolling the virtues of spirits. Other ornate gantries complete with spirit casks can be found at Bennet's Bar, Tollcross, Edinburgh and the Volunteer Arms (Staggs), Musselburgh. There is also one from the 1920s at Auldhouse Arms, Auldhouse, South Lanarkshire. Ornate gantries that have lost their spirit casks can be found at the Camphill Vaults, Bothwell and the Douglas Arms Hotel, Banchory. Other pubs with ornate gantries include the Tay Bridge Bar, Dundee, incorporating a fine mirror; the Rowan Tree, Uddingston with two glazed cigar cabinets and another from 1926 at the Grill, Aberdeen.

The impressive gantry at the Old Toll Bar, Glasgow.

At the Old Wine Store, Shotts, you can still get your whisky 'direct from the cask'.

Above right: the Bull, Paisley, there are six sets of four spirit cocks used to dispense the spirits from the casks on the gantry. These are the only ones of which we are aware in Scotland.

In the past, whisky was brought from the distillery in bulk and blended on the premises, with the finished blend transferred from pub cellars using a water engine (see page 77) to the barrels on the gantry ready to be served. While in most pubs this practice generally ceased in the interwar period, there is just one pub in Scotland where you can still get a 'dram from the cask'. At the Old Wine Store, Shotts, the blender William Morton supplied its blend in bulk until recently and the no. 3 barrel is still used for serving whisky but now it is topped-up once a fortnight by the landlord.

Pub room names

To this day, the Bridge Bar, Bridge Street, Aberdeen, one of the last men-only pubs in Scotland, has no ladies toilet, and there is a sign on the door to warn customers of the fact!

Sitting Room

Not all Scottish pubs are single spaces. There are many that retain separate rooms termed 'sitting rooms'; where they are very small, we refer to them as 'snugs'. These rooms point up the contrast between respectable seated drinking that would take place therein, as opposed to the 'stand-up drinking' to be expected in the rest of the premises. Good examples are at the Steps, Glasgow; Clep, Dundee; and the Portland Arms, Shettleston, where there are no fewer than four of them. Occasionally, these rooms can be called 'private', as can be seen in the door glass at Athletic Arms ('Diggers'), Edinburgh but, sadly, the room division here was removed recently. In the Crown, Arbroath, one room has 'Private Parlour' on the door.

Ladies' Room/Ladies' Snug

Pubs in Scottish cities and towns were overwhelmingly male-dominated and, indeed, a handful of them, most notably the Grill and the Bridge Bar in Aberdeen, remained 'men-only' until the Sex Discrimination Act became law on 1 January 1976. Up until recently, the Imperial Bar,

At the Portland Arms, Shettleston, built in 1938, the sitting room is labelled 'Ladies Room', reflecting the situation that by the 1930s women were being encouraged into the respectable surroundings of new lounge bars.

Wishaw, still continued the practice of allowing only men into the bar, while women used the 'ladies' snug' on the right of the entrance porch. It is predominately women that still use the snug in the Ritz, Cambuslang, south of Glasgow.

Family Department

There still exist a number of the tiny rooms, or booths, where drink was bought for consumption off the premises: the purchasers were often women, even children, who were sent to the pub to collect the family supplies. One of the best examples is at Bennet's Bar, Edinburgh, where it is called Jug and Bottle, so named, of course, after the vessels used to take home the chosen liquids. Other intact examples can be found at the Prestoungrange Gothenburg, Prestonpans, where it is called Jug Bar; Portland Arms, Shettleston, where it is called Family Department; and the Harbour Bar, Kirkcaldy. There is a very late one dating from the 1960s at Laurieston Bar, Glasgow, the decade when people began to stop using the pub for take-home supplies.

The jug bar at the Prestoungrange Gothenburg, Prestonpans.

The family department at the Portland Arms, Shettleston.

Office

A less frequently seen room is the owner's or manager's office, as shown on the plan of MacSorley's (see page 6). There are surviving examples still in use by staff at the Old Toll Bar, Glasgow, which retains its original colourful glass panel, and at the Links Tavern, Edinburgh. The office at the Red Lion, Kelso, is accessed through the fifth bay of the gantry, and there is a modernised one within the counter of the Horseshoe Bar, Glasgow. At Lang's, Paisley, the office was situated between the two front doors but, in recent years, it has been converted into a snug. The tiny office at the Portland Arms is now used as a cleaners' cupboard.

The office is still in use by staff at the Old Toll Bar, Glasgow.

Other Characteristics of Scottish Pubs

Brewery and Whisky Mirrors

Many Scottish (and Irish) bars are embellished with old mirrors, usually advertising long-vanished spirits and breweries/beers, as well as soft drinks and occasionally tobacco products. Some, like those at the Pittodrie Bar, Aberdeen; Barony Bar, Edinburgh; and Old Toll Bar, Glasgow, are of truly epic size.

The impressive Robert Younger's mirror at the Pittodrie Bar, Aberdeen, which has an impressive display of brewery and whisky mirrors.

Another way of advertising brewery and other products in Scottish pubs is with screens set at eye level in the front windows. Good examples can be seen at the Dalhousie, Brechin; Woodside, Falkirk; and Queens Head, Hawick. At the Town Arms, Selkirk, there are two metal screens advertising Drybrough Ales.

The bell-box in the Grapes, Stranraer, which is still in use today, indicates eight rooms – as you wander around the pub, you will find each room still retains its number.

Above right: The bell-pushes at the Horseshoe Bar, Glasgow, are of a grand style, as befits this stunning pub interior.

Bell-pushes

You will quite frequently spot bell-pushes on the walls of Scottish pubs, especially in sitting rooms. They are a reminder of the once-common practice of table service. When the bell was rung it triggered an indicator in a bell-box that was visible to bar staff. This tradition now operates in only a small number of pubs in Scotland.

In the Globe, Stranraer, table service is still available in two rooms, with the bell-box indicator on a column in the middle of the public bar. Thanks to their working bells, you can also get table service in the Steps Bar, Glasgow (sitting room); the Clep, Dundee (lounge); and Railway Tavern, Kincardine (right-hand room). On a Saturday evening only, customers in the smoke room at the Viceroy, Paisley Road West, Glasgow, can take advantage of it. At the Village Tavern, Larkhall, some customers still receive table service on a shout of 'Hoy'!

Water Taps on the Bar

Scotland is famous for whisky. Since whisky is the only spirit that can benefit from a little added water, a large numbers of counter tops had, and some still have, water taps. A few are still in working order, such as those at Bennet's Bar and Ryrie's Bar, Edinburgh; Buck Hotel, Langholm, Dumfries & Galloway; and Rowan Tree, Uddingston. Ceramic jugs bearing whisky advertising are to be found on most Scottish bars for customers to add their own water. Some Scots say 'beer is used to wash the whisky down', and this is still true in certain areas, such as the Highlands and Islands. In Glasgow, 'hauf an' a hauf pint' – a half glass of whisky and a half pint of beer, the beer being the chaser – is popular.

Water tap on the counter at Leslie's Bar, Edinburgh.

Saving the UK's Pub Heritage

CAMRA's pioneering initiative to save the nation's historic pub interiors

CAMRA's National Inventory

The Campaign for Real Ale was founded in the early 1970s to save Britain's traditional beers, which were threatened with extinction by large brewers interested only in producing bland, mass-produced beers served up under artificial gas pressure. CAMRA was incredibly successful. However, the UK's great pub heritage was being ravaged, too. The 1970s saw a massive increase in the opening up of pubs and the removal of fine fittings, many of which had stood the test of time for nearly a century. Preservation of historic pub interiors became a key issue for CAMRA.

The magnificent interior of Bennet's Bar, Edinburgh, a pub in the National Inventory Part One.

The tiled interior of the Central Bar, Leith, a pub in the National Inventory Part Two.

The first step was to identify the most intact interiors remaining among Britain's 60,000 pubs. Local pilot projects by CAMRA and the Victorian Society in the late 1970s and 1980s led to a full national survey using the knowledge of CAMRA's extensive membership. Nothing like it had been done before. Thousands of leads had to be followed up, criteria established, and different pub types and regional variations identified. The main aim was to list those interiors that remained very much as they had been before the Second World War. At the outset, it was thought that the total might be around 500 but it soon became clear that it would be nothing of the sort. After six years' work, CAMRA's first *National Inventory of Pub Interiors of Outstanding Historic Interest* (National Inventory, for short) appeared in the 1997 *Good Beer Guide*. There was a total of just 179 pubs, including 16 in Scotland, such had been the scale of modern change. Up-to-date editions of the inventory are printed in the annual *Good Beer Guide*; the latest list includes 32 pubs in Scotland.

The Next Step

The National Inventory was the first move to save the nation's historic pub interiors. CAMRA's next step has been to develop a second tier of inventories, each covering a particular part of the UK. For these, the entries have been chosen by the editors drawing upon suggestions from CAMRA members and many others. This includes local planning authorities in the region concerned, who have all been invited to contribute to the consultation process. For a pub to be included, a significant amount of genuinely historic internal fabric and/or layout must be preserved. The emphasis is on pre-1939 interiors, although post-war examples of special merit are also admitted. Interiors less than 30-years-old, however, do not qualify, as CAMRA has chosen to follow the same '30-year rule' that governs the statutory listing of a building.

Following on from the National Inventory, CAMRA's first regional inventory was for Greater London, published in 2004, and listed 133 pubs. East Anglia came out the following year, identifying 89 examples. North East England appeared in July 2006, listing 49 pubs. Guides for Yorkshire and the West Midlands are in preparation and work is also in hand for other regions. We hope the entire UK will be covered before very long.

Fiddichside Inn, Craigellachie.

Kenilworth, Edinburgh.

The descriptions in this guide aim to make clear the significance of each pub interior. Those pubs that are also featured in the National Inventory are clearly identified by the star symbols (see page 20). Additional pubs fall into one of the following categories:

- pubs with a reasonable degree of intactness in their layout and some of their fittings. Visitors should get a good idea of how the pub was originally arranged even if, for example, doors have been removed or extensions added.

- pubs where the layout has been altered more radically but where particular items or features of real importance survive.

The fact that a pub is not included in this guide does not mean it is devoid of historic value. We have had to draw the line somewhere, so you will still come across pubs with features like etched glass, old bar fittings and tile-work that are a joy to behold and deserve to be saved but they are not listed here.

Do you know of other pubs to include?

The entries for these guides draw on the accumulated knowledge of CAMRA members and we hope to have identified all the interiors worthy of inclusion. However, with so many pubs across such a vast area, there may be historic examples that have escaped our notice – if you find one, do please let us know. *Scotland's True Heritage Pubs*, like the National Inventory, is an organic document to be kept under constant review and updated in the light of feedback and further research. If you have any updates, comments or suggestions for pubs to include in future editions, please contact us at books@camra.org.uk.

The sitting room at the Central Bar, Renton.

Further reading

Geoff Brandwood, Andrew Davison & Michael Slaughter, *Licensed to Sell: The History and Heritage of the Public House* (London, 2004). A modern, well-illustrated and comprehensive survey of pub history, architecture and fittings.

Mark Girouard, *Victorian Pubs* (New Haven and London, 1984). A classic book dealing with pubs in the Victorian era; of general interest despite dealing mainly with London.

Rudolph Kenna & Anthony Mooney, *People's Palaces: Victorian and Edwardian Pubs of Scotland* (Edinburgh, 1983). A classic book dealing with the pubs of Scotland in the Victorian and Edwardian eras.

Rudolph Kenna, *The Glasgow Pub Companion* (Glasgow, 2001). A well-researched guide that includes pubs in the city with character.

Protecting Heritage Pubs

Only half of the pubs in this guide are statutorily 'listed' as buildings, meeting strict national criteria of 'architectural and historic interest'. Historic Scotland, on behalf of the Scottish Executive, has created the following three categories:

Category A   Buildings of national or international importance, either architectural or historic, or fine little-altered examples of a particular period, style or building type.

The snug bar at the Globe, Dumfries – Robert Burns's favourite pub – a Category A listed building.

Category B   Buildings of regional or more than local importance, or major examples of some particular period, style or building type which may have been altered.

Category C(s)   Buildings of local importance, lesser examples of any period, style, or building type, as originally constructed or altered; and simple, traditional buildings which group well with others in categories A and B or part of a planned group such as an estate or an industrial complex.

Listed Building Consent must be obtained where proposals will alter the character of the listed building. This applies regardless of the category of listing (A, B or C(s)) and to work affecting interior and exterior. All applications for consent are made through the local planning authority which will consider applications in the light of the advice given in Historic Scotland's Memorandum of Guidance and other national policy documents as well as their own policies. The planning authority may refer to Historic Scotland for advice at any stage during the consent process and must notify Historic Scotland of their intention to grant consent for developments affecting category A or B listed buildings and for all demolitions, regardless of category.

Being listed should offer buildings protection from damaging change. However, only four pubs featured in this guide are 'A' listed, a further 31 are 'B' listed, and 55 are unlisted.

The set of eight stained glass windows featuring British sportsmen in the Oyster Bar of the Café Royal, Edinburgh, a Category A listed building.

Many of Scotland's statutorily listed pubs do not appear in this guide. They are often listed for reasons that have nothing to do with their interiors, such as fine external appearance of the tenement building, their contribution to the urban landscape or quite simply their great age. All too often the interiors of such buildings have been so altered that they can find no place in this guide. This is a reflection of the fact that until quite recently pub interiors received little attention from mainstream planning and conservation bodies and control systems.

On the other hand there are numerous Scottish Inventory pubs that do not possess listed building status. Even though they do not meet national criteria for architectural or historic merit, they may still be significant, especially in their local context. It is often their multi-roomed interiors and range of genuine old furnishings that turn them into ideal, welcoming places for their local communities. Those communities are usually vociferous (and often effective) in protecting their pubs against unnecessary, expensive change imposed by pub-owners bent on making their entire estate conform to a stereotyped formula or 'brand'.

CAMRA firmly believes that all the pubs in *Scotland's True Heritage Pubs* are worthy of protection and sensitive treatment. We urge Historic Scotland to consider adding to the list description, the details contained within this guide, particularly where no internal description of the public house exists. Where statutory listing is lacking, we urge Historic Scotland to consider listing them and, where this is not possible, planning authorities to add the pubs to a 'local list' of historic buildings. Many authorities – but by no means all – operate such lists. They are an important way of enabling local authorities and communities to appreciate the building stock in their care. Although they have no legal force, local lists have often been a means of encouraging would-be developers to look after pubs sympathetically, thus saving them expense and preserving an asset for the community for future generations.

The 'Comm', Lochgilphead, which still retains intact its lounge and smoke room dating from a refitting in 1945, was listed Category C(s) as a result of the CAMRA project.

Feuars' Arms, Kirkcaldy, has a wonderful tiled interior but is only a Category C(s) listed building.

Barony Bar, Edinburgh – a Category B listed building – retains its original bar counter, back gantry, tiling and three massive mirrors.

Using this guide

This guide is primarily about the genuine, internal historic fabric of pubs, rather than their atmosphere or friendliness, even though these are usually found in abundance in Scotland. Inclusion in this guide is for a pub's physical attributes only, and is not to be construed as a recommendation in any other sense.

Every effort has been made to ensure the accuracy of the information at the time of going to press (January 2007), but no responsibility can be accepted for errors, and there will doubtless be changes occurring during the currency of this publication.

Real ale

If 'real ale' appears in a pub entry, it indicates that the pub sells at least one cask-conditioned beer at the time of going to press. As this is something that can change, we encourage visitors to ask for real ale where there is none on sale, as demand will result in more outlets.

Food

Many users of pub guides require details of where and when food is available. To be as helpful as possible, we have indicated where, at the time of going to press, a pub sells meals, snacks (at least toasted sandwiches, hot pies or bridies) or has a separate restaurant. If you are planning to visit a pub and require something to eat, we strongly recommend you ring in advance to check availability, as this is subject to change at short notice, particular if the licensee has changed or staff are not available.

Scottish pub culture is, historically, very different from that of England. While many English pubs are, or at least were, multi-roomed to cater for different sections of the community, Scottish pubs were mainly men-only drinking shops. It therefore stands to reason that many of the historic pubs in this guide will be of the one-room variety. Although this will not lessen your enjoyment of them, you should bear in mind that a number of them offer snacks, but some do serve full meals.

Opening hours

Most of the pubs listed here are open all day; a few are open only at lunchtimes and in the evenings, while a handful keep more restricted opening times (we have tried to give an indication of these). If in doubt or you are travelling a long distance to a particular pub, it is advisable to phone ahead to check.

Key

Listed status **Statutory listing**: whether a pub building is statutorily listed or not is spelled out, together with the grade at which it is listed (see page 17).

★ **National Inventory**: pubs on Part One of CAMRA's National Inventory of Pub Interiors of Outstanding Historic Interest, that is ones that remain wholly or largely intact since before World War Two or, in exceptional cases, built to a traditional planform up to thirty years ago.

☆ **National Inventory**: pubs on Part Two of the National Inventory, that is ones whose interiors have been altered but which retain exceptional rooms or features of national historic importance.

⇌ **Near railway station**

⊖ **Near Subway station**

🚌 **Bus routes** that regularly passes close to pubs.

CITY OF ABERDEEN

Aberdeen
6–8 Little Belmont Street
AB10 1JG
01224 644487
Not listed
⇌ Aberdeen
Meals all day (to 6.45pm Sat, Sun)
Real ale

One of the two intact snugs at
Cameron's Inn (Ma's), Aberdeen.

Cameron's Inn (Ma's)

This pub had a massive expansion in recent years but two of its three original rooms remain unscathed. There is a wood-panelled snug complete with bare bench seating, a hatch for service and two 1920s perforated bentwood seats. A partition wall, which retains two of its five original windows, separates the snug from the public bar on the left. This retains its back gantry, old counter, panelled walls and has two old leather-covered benches. Another small room on the left of the entrance has been modernised. The public bar and snug may close early if there are no customers.

Aberdeen
213 Union Street AB11 6BA
01224 573530
Category B Listed
⇌ Aberdeen
Snacks all day
Real ale

Detail on the long bar counter

Grill ★

Originally a restaurant and dining rooms from the 1870s, the Grill retained its name when it was remodelled by architects Jenkins & Marr and turned into a pub in 1926. The mainly stand-up bar retains its fittings of that date, including a finely carved mahogany back gantry with three glazed cabinets. There are over 300 single malt Scottish whiskies on sale – ask for the informative menu. Occupying the ground floor of a typical grey granite three-storey terrace property of the early 1830s, the pub has two ceiling sections with moulded plasterwork – the front, oval in shape; the rear, circular. The long mahogany carved bar counter has a number of badged sections on the front each with a letter 'G' and a brass match-striker all along it. The walls are covered in mahogany veneer and the tables with cast-iron bases are inscribed 'The Grill'. As this was a strict 'men-only' bar until the Sex Discrimination Act came into force on 1 January 1976, there was no ladies toilet until 1998 when new gents facilities were added downstairs and the former gents WC revamped into the ladies.

The stand-up bar at the Grill, Aberdeen.

Pittodrie Bar

Aberdeen
337–9 King Street AB24 5AP
01224 638836
Not Listed
🚍 1
Snacks on match days only

The only pub in Aberdeen to retain its original island-style bar, which has one of the best displays of brewery and whisky mirrors in Scotland. While not visually exciting, the original oval-shaped counter has a rare mosaic (former) spittoon trough all around the base, and a match-striker running just under the top. The island gantry has been replaced in recent years but is similar in design to the original. There are six large and two small mirrors on the walls, including a splendid one for Robert Younger's St Ann's Brewery by T J Ford of Edinburgh. A small sitting room was lost in the 1960s by the removal of a short glazed partition on the left. The pub is very busy when football is screened.

Prince of Wales

Aberdeen
7–11 St Nicholas Lane
AB10 1HF
01224 640597
Category C(s) Listed
🚆 Aberdeen
Meals lunchtimes
Real ale

This late-Victorian granite pub has two carved back gantries and, at 18m (60ft), the longest bar counter for miles around. Originally it consisted only of the right-hand half of the present-day pub but, in the 1980s, numbers 9 and 11 to the left were purchased and areas at the front and rear created. The long counter has an old spittoon trough around the base with new tiles, and the bar top has been replaced. Good collection of brewery and whisky mirrors.

The bar counter at the Prince of Wales, Aberdeen is some 60 feet in length.

Aberdeen
97 High Street,
Old Aberdeen AB23 3EN
01224 483079
Category B Listed
🚌 20
Snacks all day

St Machar Bar

In an 18th-century building, this long, narrow bar, popular with students, has remained unchanged for the past 40 years. It has a long counter and a back gantry of shelves, the lower ones of which are covered with Formica. Other 1960s fittings include the distinctive suspended canopy, the panelling on the walls and the bare wood fixed seating with a cushioned back running down the left-hand side and at the front. Prior to the 1960s there was a snug where the dartboard is now. The ladies toilets were not added until the refit.

TRY ALSO

The Blue Lamp, 121 Gallowgate (01224 647271) is also little altered since the 1960s. The U-shaped public bar was formerly two rooms. The upstairs lounge is intact having a back gantry, suspended beams over the Formica topped counter, fixed seating all from the 1960s, but this room is now only used for private functions.

ABERDEENSHIRE

Banchory
22 High Street AB31 5SR
01330 822547   Not Listed
Meals: lunchtimes and
evenings; all day in summer
Real ale

Douglas Arms

A popular pub that doubles as a hotel with a public bar that has retained its main features from a refitting of c.1900. The little-changed public bar is dominated by a long panelled counter and a corresponding gantry, the centre part of which has five bays with depressed arches. At each end of the counter there are tall, glazed display cases, and from

the back of the bar are two hatches (possibly modern insertions) to the rear games room. There are a pair of noteworthy advertising mirrors: on the left, for W B Black of Aberdeen's East India Pale Ale; on the right, for Queens Ale and Vigor Stout from Thompson Marshall (also of Aberdeen). The fixed seating has been replaced, and there are a variety of other rooms that are mostly modernised.

The public bar at the Douglas Arms Hotel, Banchory, shortly after it was refitted in c.1900 – it looks very similar today.

Stonehaven

9–10 Shorehead AB39 2JY
01569 762155
Category C(s) Listed
⇌ Stonehaven
Meals lunchtimes and evenings
Real ale

Marine

Attractively sited overlooking the harbour and built in 1884 as a
temperance hotel, the public bar remains virtually unchanged,
with fittings more likely to have been added in the early 1900s.
The completely wood-panelled bar has an original bar counter,
mirrored back gantry, benches of some considerable age, including
a curved one in the corner. The lounge on the right has been created
from an adjoining building and has no old fittings. The upstairs
dining room, with a decorative cornice and ceiling rose, has a bar
counter and associated woodwork probably installed in the 1960s.

ANGUS

Arbroath

41 West Abbey Street
DD11 1EV
01241 873824
Not Listed
⇌ Arbroath
No food

Crown Bar

A three-roomed pub with a stand-up public bar little-altered in 100
years. It retains a decorative back gantry, which, as a photo on the wall
shows, originally had spirit casks on it; the original counter has a new
top. On the panelled walls are large 'John A Bertram Co. Scotch Whisky',
'McEwan's India Pale Ale' and 'Wm Younger's' mirrors. This bar retains
its original fireplace, basic bare bench and window seating, a good
'Crown Inn Bar' window and McEwan's window screens. Leave the
public bar by the rear left door and along the passage is a small room
with a 'Private Parlour' glass panel, a long, large 'Wm Younger & Co's
India Pale Ale' mirror, c.1960s leatherette fixed seating and tables fixed
to the floor. Further down the passage is a new lounge, converted from
the adjoining house in the 1960s and retaining most of its fittings
from that date.

The little-altered public bar of the
Crown, Arbroath.

Arbroath

5–7 East Mary Street DD11 1PR
01241 872524
Not Listed
⇄ Arbroath
No food

While in Arbroath, do visit one of the many small fishmongers in the harbour area selling the mouth-watering local speciality – Arbroath smokies (hot-smoked haddock).

Foundry Bar

Single-storey, dormer-windowed drinkers' pub with three rooms, that has been in operation since 1861. The small bar retains its original counter with a series of painted panels interspersed with Swan Vesta match-strikers. On top of the counter is a wooden gantry some 50 years old that reaches to the ceiling. There is a modest original back gantry on the left; on the right was the former off-sales. The walls retain their original panels and the old fireplace has a lintel with the date 1775. Look for the gauge on the wall from the days when the beer was raised from the cellar to the bar by mains water pressure (see page 77). The lounge at the rear retains its old panelled walls with bell-pushes at the front; it was extended back in the late 1980s to twice its original size. On the left, two small rooms have been converted to a games room, which retains some old bench seating.

Brechin

62 Market Street DD9 6BD
01356 622813
Not Listed
Meals lunchtimes and evenings

Brown Horse Hotel

Former hotel retaining three small, little-altered rooms, with a lounge added in the 1960s, also barely changed. The original entrance door has a colourful pictorial glass panel and leads to a very small bar with fittings that may date from the early 20th century. The bar counter has a match-striker under the lip, and the back gantry features one large 'Bell's Perth Whisky' mirror centrepiece and four smaller whisky mirrors around it, two on each side. This half-panelled stand-up man's bar has no tables, just a couple of stools. There are small rooms to the left and rear still with a few old fittings. The lounge added in 1966 retains its solid counter, bar back panelling, typical 1960s plank canopy and offset seating bays, which, while not visually exciting, are rare. The outside gents has been retained.

Brechin

1 Market Street DD9 6BA
01356 622096
Category B Listed
No food

Dalhousie

Town centre drinkers' pub in a three-storey building from 1879 in mid-Victorian Renaissance style with a public bar not changed in 50 years. The high-ceilinged public bar has original full-height panelled walls and a horseshoe-shaped counter that could be of 1950/60s vintage, both of which have had their dark stain removed in recent years and replaced by a light one. This pub not only has an old carved back gantry but also a modest island gantry, possibly a 1950/60s addition, which is on wheels and has to be moved to gain access to the cellar below. Good 1930s windows include one etched 'Afternoon Teas' and three old window screens – one is in a frame on the wall; another reads 'Breakfast Luncheons High Teas'. Nowadays only crisps and nuts are available! The small pool room has no old fittings.

ARGYLL & BUTE

Lochgilphead

Lochnell Street
01546 602492
Category C(s)
No food

'It's open when it's closed, and it's closed when it's open' – this door at The 'Comm', Lochgilphead opens to both the smoke room and the serving area.

The 'Comm' ★

An early 19th-century building that was refitted in 1945–6 and retains a rare, untouched post-war interior of three rooms, and includes a door that's open when it's closed and closed when it's open! The small drinkers' public bar has a curved panelled bar with fluted pilasters and a gantry with mirrored display shelves. Other original fittings include the brick-built fireplace with brick canopy, Art Deco mirror above and timber wall benches. Along a passage and through the multi-pane door is the smoke room with a small stepped fire surround and more wall bench seating. Continuing to the rear, you will find the lounge with bench seating separated by curvilinear partitions, a large fireplace with a brick canopy and the original tables. The tiny gents toilet has a sliding door with 'Gents Lavatory – Slide it Chum' inscribed in red on a cut-glass panel.

Rothesay, Isle of Bute

3 East Princes Street PA20 9DL
01700 502095
Category B Listed
Ferry: Wemyss Bay to Rothesay
No food

The partitioned snug at the Golfer's Bar, Rothesay, Isle of Bute.

Golfers' Bar

This drinkers' pub, which occupies the ground floor of a tenement built in 1901, still retains most of its refitting from *c*.1930 in Glasgow Art Nouveau style. The public bar has an impressive mirrored gantry with stained glass cupboard fronts and ten drawers, a long bar counter and extensive panelling. At the front there is a snug accessed via sliding doors with etched windows and partition walls. Around the public bar, just below the floral frieze, there is a series of painted plans depicting all the holes at Rothesay golf course. The pub is situated close to the ferry terminal, where you will find the most impressive surviving late-Victorian gents public toilets in the UK.

DUMFRIES & GALLOWAY

Annan

10 High Street DG12 6AG
01461 202385
Category C(s) Listed
⇌ Annan
No food
Real ale

Blue Bell

In 1917, all the pubs in Annan became part of the Gretna State
Management Scheme, one of a handful of such schemes in the UK,
and they continued to be owned by the government until 1972.
The idea was to control the consumption of alcohol by workers in
the munitions factories at Gretna and, under the scheme, the Blue
Bell was refitted and it has not changed much since. This former
coaching inn, where Hans Christian Anderson is said to have
stayed, dates back to 1770, but the red sandstone building is now
mainly mid-19th century, although it still retains its stables at the
rear. The main change in the last 50 years has been the removal of
a sliding screen on the left of the entrance, which gives the pub an
open-plan feel. All the walls are covered in inter-war panelling, as
is the bar counter, but the counter top and back gantry have been
replaced in the past 30-odd years. There was a tiny snug on the
right-hand side until the 1970s. The gents is intact with a panelled
ante-room, tiled inner room and original Shanks urinals.

Dumfries

56 High Street DG1 2JA
01387 252335
www.globeinndumfries.co.uk
Category A Listed
⇌ Dumfries
Meals lunchtimes and evenings
Real ale

Globe Inn

Dumfries is famous for its connections with Scotland's patriot bard
Robert Burns, and the Globe Inn is known as the Burns Howff, i.e. his
favourite pub. This mid-18th-century brick building is situated down
a narrow wynd (alley) off the High Street. It contains a number of
Burns artefacts, and tours are offered at quiet times (so avoid 12 to 3).
Opposite the entrance is a sliding door that leads into the old panelled
snug bar, created by wooden partition walls with bench seating

The former kitchen in the Globe,
Dumfries, now in use as a dining
room.

attached. The snug retains its old back gantry of shelves on tongue-and-grooved walls and bar counter, although it has a replacement top. The main bar at the rear was extended back in the 1980s to just over twice its original size, while the counter was installed in the 1980s. At the front of the pub are two small 18th-century panelled rooms brought into use as dining rooms in recent years. The first has a black-leaded range fireplace and some bench seating. Robert Burns' favourite chair situated in the front room of the Globe, Dumfries. If you sit in it local custom states that you have to recite one of his poem's or your forfeit is to buy everyone in the pub a drink! The Burns bedroom upstairs has etchings on two windowpanes that have been authenticated as being written by Burns. If you want to find out more about Burns, visit the nearby Robert Burns House, which is on the way to the Ship Inn.

Robert Burns' favourite chair

Dumfries
97 St Michael Street DG1 2PY
01387 255189
Not Listed
⇌ Dumfries
No food
Real ale

Ship Inn

Situated opposite St Michael's churchyard, where you will find Burns's mausoleum, is this small three-roomed pub that has been little altered in 40 years. It was converted from an early Victorian house into a two-roomed pub with snugs in *c.*1900. A vestibule entrance leads into the small public bar, which has an original mirrored back gantry with a modern piece at the top. The original bar counter has a panelled frontage, probably added in the 1960s, and a new top. Prior to 1960, there was a row of three snugs down the left side and another on the front right. Horizontal panelled walls probably date from the 1960s. Continuing to the rear, you will find a lounge with fittings from the late 1960s, including panelled walls and a fireplace. Both the public bar and lounge retain their highly decorative Victorian plasterwork cornices and ceiling roses. Beyond the gents is a small room brought into use in recent years. Good stained glass and leaded 'ship' front windows.

Langholm
17 High Street DG13 0JH
01387 380400
Category C(s) Listed
No food

Buck Hotel

Mid 18th-century small hotel that has been modernised but retains its narrow public bar with two old back gantries. On the left the gantry has a mirrored back and two narrow mirror strips, while the one on the right has slender supports and holds 50 single malt whiskies. The bar counter with two sets of disused beer engine handles and a working water tap is at least 50 years old and curves in front of the right gantry. Other old features include the panelled walls and ceiling, a 100-year-old cast-iron and glazed brick fireplace but the seating is modern. The front door leads into a Victorian tiled hallway with an old bell-box and a hatch for service. The sitting room at the rear was converted to a lounge in the early 1970s; on the left is a modernised games room, which was formerly two small rooms.

Stranraer

4–6 Bridge Street DG9 7HY

01776 703386

Not Listed

⇌ Stranraer

No food

The working bell-box in the Grapes, Stranraer,

The 1930's Art Deco gantry and counter in the upstairs bar.

Grapes ★

Town centre pub little altered in 50 years and now coming up again after years of decline. Originally a coaching inn, the present building was erected in 1862 and still has the former stables at the rear. The mainly stand-up bar has a gantry at least 100 years old, incorporating a brewery mirror, a 1950s bar counter front with a new top, tongue-and-groove panelled walls and old fixed seating. Opposite the bar counter is a working bell-box, and it is still possible to get table service in the two small rear sitting rooms at any time of the day. Each room has large plain mirrors on the walls and refurbished fixed seating, but a third small room has been converted to an office. Note the numbers on the doors: '1' for the bar, '3' and '7' on the sitting rooms, and '4' on the office. Upstairs the lounge with '6' on the door has a 1930s Art Deco gantry and counter that came from a hotel in Ayr in the 1950s. The fittings have some modern extensions to make them fit in this room, which is said to be the first cocktail bar in Stranraer and still has its original chairs. There is a tiny room off the lounge with '5' on the door and another room numbered '8' now just forms part of the route to the ladies toilet.

CITY OF DUNDEE

Broughty Ferry

10–12 Fort Street DD5 2AD

01382 775941

Category C(s) Listed

🚌 Travel Dundee 7/8, 10/9,
   10X/9X Strathtay 73, 75, 76

Meals lunchtimes and evenings

Real ale

Fisherman's Tavern

Early 19th-century former house, licensed since 1857, that has evolved from a traditional terraced pub into a small town hotel in recent years. The low-ceilinged public bar on the right is separated from the snug on the left by a low, part-glazed partition. The modest back gantry on the right is old but the one on the left is modern, while the bar counter has a 1950/60s ply frontage. The public bar has original tongue-and-grooved panelled walls, a good Bernard's mirror, 1950/60s fixed seating and a curious small table with wooden sides that was designed for a ship. At the rear in an extension is a lounge with a bar counter at least 40 years old, a highly decorative back gantry that has come from another pub, and a fine fireplace. The snug on the left has a 1930s tiled fireplace but the bar counter is modern. In a recent expansion to the left, there is a new dining room. One of few pubs in Scotland to have always sold real ale, it has appeared in practically every *Good Beer Guide*.

Dundee
96–8 Clepington Road
DD3 7SW
01382 858953
Category B Listed
🚌 7/8, 18
No food

Clep ★

Behind the unprepossessing, single-storey exterior there is this wonderfully preserved gem that gives a perfect impression of how small, urban Scottish pubs were constructed in the late 1930s. It was purpose-built together with two shops in 1940–1, and the layout of public bar, lounge, and jug and bottle is just as it was. There are working bell-pushes in all three rooms, and those in the lounge are still responded to with table service. The public bar is U-shaped around a tiled fireplace with the toilets behind (note the amazingly narrow entrance doors). It has three-quarter-height panelled walls throughout the original bar counter and back gantry. The fixed bench seating has a number of solid wooden dividers, and the tables are original. The totally unaltered small lounge has partitions forming seating bays, more panelling and leaded windows, including one advertising 'Bernard's Edinburgh Ales'. Wood-panelled passages with terrazzo floor into both the public bar and the off-sales on the right, which is still open except in cold weather.

The unaltered main bar
in the Clep, Dundee

Dundee

117 Strathmartine Road
DD3 7SD
01382 810975
Not Listed
🚌 1A, 1B, 22/22C
Snacks all day

Frew's Bar ★

A three-roomed pub with a public bar dated 1915 and two lounge bars, one of which is a rare Art Deco survivor. Situated at the foot of a three-storey tenement building, it has the metal windows typical of inter-war work: those on the corner include a plough motif in stained and leaded glass, as this was the old name of the pub. The public bar has been amalgamated with a tiny snug on the right by the removal of a short partition. Written on the back of one of the pots that decorate the inglenook-style fireplace is 'H & F Thomson Architect', 'Alex Fair Wood Carver', 'John Scott Joiner' and 'Mr Stewart Licence Holder 18th October 1915'. The back gantry with bevelled mirror panels could also date from 1915; the oblong panels and top have been added in recent years, while the counter and wall-panelling seem relatively modern. On the right is a lounge with sleek inter-war wood-panelled walls with brass bell-pushes all around but the counter was added post-war. The real star at this pub is on the left with a separate entrance in Moncur Crescent. This second lounge now celebrates sporting memories. It retains its 1930s Art Deco panelled walls, brass-stepped quarter-circle bar, counter front and back gantry, fireplace, fixed seating and even the tables.

The Sporting Memories lounge at Frew's Bar, Dundee is open only Friday nights and on Saturday, or by prior appointment.

Dundee

91–3 Strathmartine Road
DD3 7QY
01382 858477
Not Listed
🚌 1A, 1B, 22/22C
No food

Glenlivet Bar

A basic drinkers' pub with a little-altered 1950s interior. The public bar has panelled walls, a stepped counter front (the top is new) and a straightforward mirrored back gantry. On the right, a sitting room, minus its door and with a glass panel recently placed in the partition wall is now used for darts. The small sitting room on the left remains intact with panelled walls, bell-pushes, door and fixed seating. Both the ladies and the gents are unchanged with terrazzo floors and walls. In the late 1990s, a former sweet shop on the right was converted into a new lounge bar. In 2003, one-third of the bar back was cut through to make it easier for the bar staff to see customers waiting for service in the lounge.

Dundee

165–7 Perth Road DD1 1AS

01382 667783

Category B Listed

⇌ Dundee

🚌 Travel Dundee 9X/10X;
Strathtay 75, 76

Snacks all day

Real ale

Speedwell Tavern (Mennie's) ★

This pub has one of the finest intact Edwardian pub interiors in the country. The original mahogany multi-bay back gantry faces two ways at right angles and holds some 160 single malt whiskies. Mennie's, named after the family that ran the pub for 50 years, was built in 1903 by architects John Bruce & Son for William Speed & Sons on the ground floor of a Scottish Baronial-style, four-storey tenement building. The bar is split into two by a low, part-glazed screen with a door in the middle. The L-shaped mahogany bar counter has three other short glazed partitions attached and an old terrazzo spittoon trough around the base. The bar has dado panelled walls and a decorative Anaglypta Jacobean ceiling, which was originally painted red but has been changed to white following the introduction of the smoking ban in Scotland. It retains its original fireplace, good cornice work, a pargetted frieze and a bell-push. On the left side are two sitting rooms with a glazed screen between them. They both have original dado panelling, fireplaces and some bell-pushes, but the seating is modern. The vestibule entrance, doors and partitions have etched glass panels, a number of which are original. Even the toilets retain their original large Shanks 'Odourless' urinals, original cistern, white tiled walls and mosaic floor.

The Edwardian Speedwell Bar, Dundee has barely altered in over 100 years.

Dundee

127–9 Perth Road DD1 4JD
01382 643973
Not Listed
⇌ Dundee
🚌 Travel Dundee 9X/10X;
   Strathtay 75, 76
No food

Tay Bridge ★

This pub has an original Victorian public bar, an Art Deco lounge and a third bar in a former shop. The public bar has an original back gantry that incorporates a number of mirrors, including a splendid one depicting the Tay railway bridge. Other original features include the bar counter, Lincrusta ceiling, ornate ceiling roses and cornices. There is a snug on the left separated by a low, glazed partition and with a sliding hatch to the bar. Go through a door on the right to the beautiful walnut-panelled lounge bar with Art Deco detailing, which is just as it was in the 1930s, apart from the glazed partition at the rear, which is a replica. The bar counter has a carved front, traditional brass foot rail, a former spittoon trough made of terrazzo around the base and an emery paper strip for striking matches under the counter lip. Look for the telephone box subtly hidden behind the panelling by the door to the bar (the telephone has long gone). On the far right is a lounge with an Art Deco feel to it, which was converted from a cobbler's shop in post-war times and undoubtedly designed to match the Walnut Lounge. On the wall is a large poster print of the Tay railway bridge by the famous railway artist Terence Cuneo – can you find the trademark mouse that he includes in all his paintings?

Left: The 1930s elegant Walnut Bar at the Tay Bridge Bar, Dundee.

The mirrored back gantry and tiny snug in the public bar at the Tay Bridge Bar, Dundee.

EAST AYRSHIRE

Kilmarnock
22–4 West George Street
KA1 1DG
No phone
Not Listed
≉ Kilmarnock
Meals lunchtimes

Fanny by Gaslight

Very much a young persons' rock music pub with bands on Friday nights, but still of historic interest behind the gaudy paint and dim lighting. Formerly the Fifty Waistcoats and originally the Railway Tavern, the pub was remodelled by Charles H Robinson in 1903, when a massive, oval-shaped bar counter with large-scale plain detailing and a low, three-tier island gantry were installed. In 1980, the bar was reduced by 2.5m (8ft) on either side, otherwise the room is largely intact with four cast-iron columns with florid Corinthian capitals supporting the beams for the upper floor. The rear snug and office are no longer in use. The large lounge upstairs was turned into a flat in the mid-1980s.

EAST DUNBARTONSHIRE

Bishopriggs
130 Kirkintolloch Road
G64 2LT
0141 762 0655
Not Listed
≉ Bishopbriggs
🚌 88, 175
No food

Quin's Bar

Large, basic, high-ceilinged Edwardian bar with a small snug. The public bar has an attractive pedimented back gantry with mirrored panels, a clock and some modern additions. The original bar counter has lost its old spittoon trough, and there are four columns with ornate capitals picked out in gold. A sitting room on the left was absorbed into the bar by the removal of part of the adjoining wall in the late 1990s. On the right-hand side of the pub is the separate family department, which was in operation until 1994 and is now a snug with old seating.

EAST LOTHIAN

Musselburgh
10 Ravensheugh Road
EH21 7PR
0131 665 3220
Not Listed
≉ Wallyford
🚌 Lothian 26, 44, 44A &
   First 66 (Sun), 129
Meals lunchtimes & evenings
Real ale

Levenhall Arms

Three-roomed pub on the east side of town close to the racecourse and popular with locals and racegoers. Formerly a coaching inn dating back to 1830, it was refitted in 1953 and has changed little since. The bar on the left retains its lapped wood counter, mirrored gantry, beauty board panelled walls and two stone fireplaces now with radiators in front. There is a separate small games room at the rear. The lounge on the right, which was formerly two small rooms and a snug, had a gantry added in 1953 and a bar counter and fixed seating in the 1970s.

Musselburgh

78–81 North High Street
EH21 6JE
0131 665 9654
Not Listed
⇌ Mussleburgh
🚌 Lothian 26, 30, 44, 44A &
   First 44, 44B, 44C, 66 (Sun),
   129
Own food allowed
Real ale

The re-sited jug bar doors

Volunteer Arms (Staggs)

A small back-street pub dating from 1858 and still owned by the same family. It has a barely altered, dimly lit bar with dark tongue-and-grooved panelled walls and segmented ceiling. The bar counter is original but with a new Formica top. The late-Victorian back gantry with four polished huge spirit casks on top is an unusual survivor. The right-hand door did lead to the jug bar but this has been removed and a 'Jug Bar' half-door panel moved to the main inner doors. There are glazed baffles at each end of the seating, old window screens, original 'Young & Co's Pale Ale Fisherrow Edinburgh' and 'Wm Whitelaw & Son's Pale Ale' mirrors. At the end of the bar counter there is a sliding door that contains a shelf for drinks and is widely used by drinkers standing in the panelled passage. Beyond the bar is a sitting room called the bar lounge that, up to 50 years ago, was two snugs. A new lounge at the rear was added post-war and refitted in the early 1990s.

North Berwick

19 Forth Street EH39 4HX
01620 892692
Not Listed
⇌ North Berwick
No food
Real ale

Auld House

Built in 1894, this town centre pub has a little altered high-ceilinged bar with a spirit barrel gantry and two other rooms. The public bar retains its original three-bay mirrored gantry with carved pillars and six old spirit barrels perched on the top, but the bar counter was replaced in the early 1980s. Other old features include the two tall front windows with pictorial etched panels, panelled walls and a good cornice. A small, little-used darts room behind the bar is served by a hatch. The left-hand side lounge was originally two rooms and is much modernised.

Prestonpans

227–9 High Street EH32 9BE
01875 819922
Category B Listed
⇌ Prestonpans
🚌 Lothian 26, First 129, 66 (Sun)
Meals lunchtimes & evenings
Real ale

Prestoungrange Gothenburg ☆

This pub is of great importance, both for its superb Edwardian fittings and because it is run along Gothenburg lines (see page 70). It was built in 1908 of red sandstone for the East of Scotland Public Houses Trust in Arts and Crafts style and still retains its Art Nouveau interior. The pub was sold to the London-based Trust Houses Ltd in 1919 and then in 1965 to Bass, when it was run as a conventional commercial pub. By the mid-1990s, it was failing, and in 2001, it was closed but passed

The Prestoungrange Gothenburg, Prestonpans, has a beautiful Arts & Crafts-style interior.

Wall tiling from 1908 at the Prestoungrange Gothenburg, Prestonpans.

into the hands of the present enlightened ownership. After meticulous restoration, it re-opened in 2003 and won the CAMRA national conservation award for the quality of the work. The public bar is a wonderful room with superbly designed features – low, segmental arches at the sides with vertical struts, deep green tiles, panelling and a spectacular jug bar. The latter includes a tiny cubicle (with a seat on the right) in front of the entrance lobby and woodwork of considerable intricacy. To the left is an elegantly panelled lounge used mainly for food and non-alcoholic refreshments. Since 2001, the building has been extended at the rear to include a small brewery (opened May 2004). There are further rooms upstairs all with modern fittings.

Tranent
131 Church Street EH33 1BL
01875 610200
Not Listed
⇄ Tranent
🚌 Lothian 26 (15, 15a) &
    First 44B, 44C
No food

Tower Inn
A single-storey terracotta stone pub built in 1902 and still with a lot of original fittings in the stand-up bar. It has a splendid three-bay back gantry incorporating a large 'Livingstone's Malt Whisky' mirror in the centre. The pub has been subject to two significant refurbishments. Shortly after long-serving licensee James Inglis took over in 1948, a jug bar and snug on the right were removed, the long bar counter shortened and some ply panelling added to the walls of the bar. In addition, a lounge, complete with a new small counter and gantry, was created in the room on the left. New owners in 2002 refurbished the lounge and removed the 1950s bar counter and gantry. There is a good collection of brewery and whisky mirrors.

CITY OF EDINBURGH

New Town

3–5 Rose Street EH2 2PR

0131 225 5276

Category B Listed

⇌ Waverley

🚌 Princes Street buses

Meals lunchtimes; restaurant
lunchtimes and evenings

Real ale on Aitken fonts

Abbotsford ★

One of the finest examples of an island-style pub built in 1902 and
barely altered since. It is owned by Jenner's, Edinburgh's famous
department store. It is believed to have been built by Charles Jenner so
that his workmen could spend their wages in his own establishment!
Unlike the majority of pubs in this style, the Abbotsford has no island
gantry. Instead, there is a carved mahogany structure with a balustrade
around the top perched on the bar counter, similar to a modern day
'pot shelf' – Leslie's Bar (see page 77) has a similar arrangement.
Designed by one of Edinburgh's most prolific pub architects, Peter Lyle
Henderson, it is a red sandstone ashlar building with a corner turret.
In the far left corner is the original snack counter, an unusual survivor

The Abbotsford is one of only a
handful of pubs in Edinburgh still
using the traditional Scottish
method of dispense – the tall fount
(the 'u' is silent) – to dispense its
range of real ales (see page 47).

The small 'snack bar' at the
Abbotsford, Edinburgh.

still in use for ordering meals at lunchtime, with a good back gantry with a balustrade and bevelled mirrored panels. The dark dado-panelled walls have inlaid mirrors, there are mahogany fittings including pediments above the doors, and a very decorative high ceiling in green and cream painted plaster. There was a small lounge at the rear of bar but this was lost when the first floor was acquired for pub use in the early 1970s and a staircase built in its place. The upstairs restaurant has quality fittings, including a small circular bar counter and panelled walls with inset mirrors but all date from the 1970s.

Leith
1–2 Yardheads EH6 6BU
0131 467 7109
Not Listed
🚌 1, 7, 10, 14, 21, 22, 34
No food

Anderson's Bar (Ghillies)

Small pub still with two sitting rooms and unusual in that customers can stand within the servery area. It is situated in the bottom of a tenement dated 1886 and little altered due to having only four owners since it opened as a pub. The long, narrow dado-panelled public bar has a counter at least 100 years old with a new top and a gantry with an old lower half but a top half that was replaced 30 years ago. Behind the counter at the rear of the bar there is a fireplace now covered over. Even today you will find customers in this area, although there is no coal fire to attract them, and the counter is used by customers to play dominoes. The left-hand door leads to a tiny jug bar but the partition door was removed c.1988 and only a small part of the screen on the counter top remains; originally there was a hatch. The front sitting room on the right retains its ply panelling, 1960s fixed seating and two-level red Formica top tables.

Dalry
1–3 Angle Park Terrace
EH11 2JX
0131 337 3822
Category C(s) Listed
🚌 1, (2), 3, 3A, (4), 25, 33, 34, 35, 44. 44A
Snacks all day
Real ale, most on Aitken founts

Athletic Arms (Diggers)

'A shadow of its former self' is how some local people describe the Diggers, the name coming from the pub's position between two large cemeteries. However, its layout is much as it was. Situated on the ground floor of an 1889 five-storey tenement block, the pub was owned by the T W Innes Trust from 1899 and remained unchanged until purchased by Scottish & Newcastle in the mid 1990s. The changes in recent years include the replacement of the bar counter, a new bar top and, in 2002, the removal of the partitions that formed the separate jug bar and private bar, as well as the solid wooden screen from the top of the bar counter and a set of three tall founts (see page 77). Only the back gantry of sturdy well-carved wood, the small island gantry of oak and the screened office area created by two low partition walls at the rear are original. Away to the right, separated by a glazed screen, is the small back room with tongue-and-groove timber dado and brass service bells. The pub gets packed for Hearts home matches and rugby matches at nearby Murrayfield.

New Town

81–3 Broughton Street EH1 3RJ
0131 558 2874
Category B Listed
🚌 8; London Road buses;
    Leith Walk buses
Meals lunchtimes and evenings
    (Sun to 7pm)
Real ale

Barony Bar

Small, L-shaped single-bar pub with a splendid interior that is well worth the short walk from the city centre. Situated in an 1804 four-storey tenement, it wraps around other property on a street corner and has an attractive frontage of teak. The public bar is notable for its 1899 decorative scheme by John Forrester, with colourful wall-tiling, a couple of massive mirrors advertising MacLaughlan Bros' wares and, around the corner, a Wm Younger's mirror. The bar counter and back gantry of oak, pedimented with mirrors and ornamental balustrades, are original. The pub not only has two Victorian tiled fireplaces with fine mirrored overmantels but also decorative ceiling brackets and cornice. Originally, the right-hand front door led to a jug and bottle and there were a couple of snugs at the rear.

The tiled dado at the Barony Bar, Edinburgh includes four tiled panels of rural Scottish scenes.

Tollcross
8 Leven Street EH3 9LG
0131 229 5143
Category B Listed
🚌 10, 11, 16, 23, 27
Meals lunchtimes and evenings
Real ale

The superb arcading at
Bennet's Bar, Edinburgh

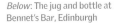

Below: The jug and bottle at
Bennet's Bar, Edinburgh

Bennet's Bar ★

Edinburgh's second finest interior after the Café Royal and little changed since 1906. It is the last pub in the city with an original gantry featuring four spirit casks, and has a wonderful tiled and mirrored interior, as well as a rare jug bar. It also stocks 120 single malt whiskies. The ornate gantry has niches, pilasters and scallop shell pediments. The original bar counter retains a former spittoon trough made of marble, which runs all along the front, and the bar top has two working brass water taps. Designed in 1891 by George Lyle, the pub has a fine ceiling with very decorative cornices, and it was refitted in 1906.

The magnificent interior features an extraordinary four-bay mirrored arcading all the way down the right-hand side, with hand-painted pictorial tiles with allegorical figures by William B Simpson & Sons of London. Below the arcading are red leather seating areas and tables inlaid with maps, some of the city and some of Scotland. On the left by the entrance is the intact tiny jug and bottle, complete with hatch, one of the few left in the city. In 2002, S&N removed the office created by a carved wood screen perched on top of the bar counter on the right. There are superb leaded and stained glass windows as well as door panels advertising 'Jeffrey's Lager & W & J Jenkinson's Bottled Beers & Aerated Waters, Leith'. There are a number of coloured and gilded engraved advertising mirrors for Bernard's, Usher's, Campbell's, Taylor Macleod & Co and Bell's Perth Whisky. Other changes have been the removal of a snug at the rear, while a former sitting room at the rear is now used as an office. At the rear right is the Green Room, which was added in 1906. Accessed from Valleyfield Street, it has an ornate bar counter and gantry, but both are modern.

41

Morningside

1 Maxwell Street EH10 5HT
0131 447 1903
Not Listed
🚌 5, 11, 16, 23, 41
Rolls only
Real ale on Aitken founts

Bennet's Bar (Wee Bennet's)

The Second World War knocked the British economy for six and there was little or no money available for pub developments for a decade after 1945. When they did start up again, they were usually low key and built of economical materials. Most have now been swept away, so Wee Bennet's is, in its way, an interesting survivor of *c.*1960. (The White Horse, 266 Canongate, Old Town is another pub refitted around the same time and barely altered since.) Everything is clean and simple, with a boarded, tapering counter front and a gantry arrangement of ply backing and glass shelves. Above it, there is a suspended, illuminated hood, a popular feature in inter-war cocktail bars and then in less glamorous post-war pubs. There is some fixed seating against the walls. This unaltered pub is currently closed on Sundays.

New Town

West Register Street EH2 2AA
0131 556 1884
Category A Listed
🚆 Waverley
🚌 Princes Street buses
Meals all day; Oyster Bar
    restaurant lunchtimes and
    evenings
Real ale

Café Royal ☆

This is one of Edinburgh's most famous pubs. Its stunning interior includes nine Doulton's tiled murals, seven are of famous inventors, each at the moment of their discovery. Built in 1862 and a pub since 1901, the main Circle Bar has a white marble floor, panelled dado, foliate Rococo-style frieze and delightful compartmented ceiling. The original majestic octagonal island serving counter, which dated

The six Doulton Lambeth faïence tiled murals, designed was John Eyre, situated in the Circle Bar feature 'William Caxton, citizen of London who brought printing into England 1476'; 'Benjamin Franklin, printer distinguished in science and politics'; 'Robert Peel makes his first experiment in calico printing'; 'Michael Faraday, discoverer of electro-magnetism'; 'George Stephenson'; and 'James Watt inventor of the condensing engine & his partner Matthew Bolton'.

The three tiled murals in the Oyster Bar are of 'Louis J. M. Daguerre, scenepainter & Joseph Nicephore Niepce, joint discoverers of photography'; also two designed by Esther Lewis of a Liverpool paddle steamer and the Cunard liner Umbria, which was built in the Govan shipyard on the Clyde

from 1901 was replaced in 1979 by an equally ornate one, and a new high gantry was installed in 2002. The original fine marble fireplace with a very elaborate overmantel is still there, as are leather seating areas. Beyond a 1901 ornately carved walnut screen with a number of bevelled and engraved mirror panels by John Taylor & Son of Princess Street lies the Oyster Bar. Three of the tiled murals are in this upmarket restaurant along with eight superb large stained glass windows of British sportsmen by Ballantine & Gardiner. It still retains the original counter of red marble, and there are small tiled panels on the bar front and behind the bar. Other features of note are the grey and white diamond-shaped, marble-tiled floor, a scrolled frieze, an elaborate ceiling with gilt embellishments, a revolving door installed in the 1920s and fine original fittings in the gents downstairs, approached by a marble staircase.

0131 557 4792

Café Royal Bistro Bar

From an entrance on the west side of the building, a staircase leads to what is now a separate business on the first floor. Refitted in 1923 by J McIntyre Hendry, the interior is very little changed with a series of rooms and high, opulent plasterwork ceilings. The large bar has walls decorated with deep relief crown patterns in plasterwork picked out in gold, and an original gantry with bevelled mirrored panels, but the bar counter has a new top. Two small, wood-panelled rooms on the right are separated by a carved wood partition; the second room has a small counter, gantry and fireplace all from the 1920s. There is a further larger room and, altogether, there are three domed ceilings. Even the ladies has marble tiled walls and the gents a tiled dado. The bar is due to reopen in April 2007 after refurbishment, so please note that changes may have been made. The nearby Guildford Arms has a very elaborate Jacobean painted ceiling with spectacular cornices and friezes, a fine example of Victorian Rococo. However, the ornate bar fittings date from only 1970.

The first-floor bar of the Café Royal, Edinburgh.

Morningside
237 Morningside Road
EH10 4QU
0131 447 1484
Category B Listed
🚌 5, 11, 16, 23, 41
Meals lunchtimes and evenings
Real ale

Canny Man's

Famous multi-roomed pub with walls obscured from skirting board to ceiling with a vast collection of memorabilia accumulated over the years that impart a unique atmosphere. Visitors should carefully note the sign 'Dress casual but smart' on entering via the door in Canaan Street. Officially the Volunteer Arms, the pub was built as a two-storey private house of local grey stone, and it is still in the same family ownership since becoming a pub in 1879. The main bar at the front of the building has an old bar counter and back gantry. On the front left is a tiny area but there is no indication that it was ever a separate snug. In the early 1960s, the rooms at the front were partially opened-up and a second counter added at the rear right. A couple of small rooms have also been brought into use. This quirky pub sells its own blended whisky and over 200 single malt whiskies; it even has a champagne menu. When not busy, drinks are occasionally served on a tray with some complimentary peanuts – the prices reflect this.

Old Town
4 South College Street
EH8 9AA
0131 668 2312
Category B Listed
🚌 Nicholson Street buses
No food
Real ale

Captain's Bar

A small, basic but friendly drinkers' pub that retains its original back gantry running the length of the room with an unusual kink in the middle. This long narrow bar situated in a five-storey, *c.*1790 tenement block has old dado panelled walls and a fine 'James Gray Whiskies' mirror. The original full-length counter was replaced by a much shorter one in the 1960/70s and has two water taps that still work but are not used. At the front right of the pub is a small area that was originally a separate snug with its own entrance door.

Leith
7–9 Leith Walk EH7 5QH
0131 467 3925
Category B Listed
🚌 7, 10, 12, 14, 16, 21, 22,
    34, 35, (49)
No food

Central Bar ☆

Without doubt, one of Scotland's most stunning pub interiors. Entrance porches (with mosaic flooring and colourful stained and leaded windows) either side lead into a room whose walls are completely covered with tiles by Minton Hollins, including four tiled

The back gantry at the Central Bar, Leith features four carved griffins.

44

The four tiled panels depicting sporting scenes – yacht racing, hare-coursing, golf and shooting – on the walls of the Central Bar, Leith.

panels of sporting scenes and tall, narrow mirrors. Built in 1899 and designed by P L Henderson, this tall, nearly square space served as the bar for Leith Central station, which closed *c.*1950. The U-shaped counter backs onto a stunning light oak gantry, which has glazed cupboards for displaying cigars etc., and includes the figures of four griffins. There is also an island gantry. The counter and tabletops date from *c.*2003. On the left are four U-shaped seating areas with conventional fixed seating on the right. The ceiling is Jacobean papier-mâché, and there is a tiled frieze in an elaborate scroll pattern. Window screens with coloured glass bearing the name of John Doig (the first proprietor of the Central Bar) appear prominently on other (modern) items around the pub. There were two sitting rooms at the back originally but these have been converted to store rooms in recent years. Opens at 9am Monday to Saturday.

New Town

142 Dundas Street EH3 5DO
0131 556 1067
Not Listed
🚌 23, 27
Snacks all day
Real ale

Clark's Bar

As this guide went to press, Clark's was still a traditional, no-frills bar with two small sitting rooms at the rear. However, there are possible changes that would destroy the historic interior and make this pub look much like thousands of others. We hope they can be revised. In the base of a tenement, this basic bar was converted from a shop in 1899 and it has a high ceiling, good cornices and old dado panelling. There was originally a circular bar counter but changes in the 1960s saw the gantry moved to the right-hand wall and the current bar counter installed. The gantry was subsequently replaced in 1990, and there are a number of mirrors on the walls, some of which are old. The two small wood-panelled sitting rooms have seating probably dating from the 1960s, as well as bell-pushes.

Portobello

36 Portobello High Street
EH15 1DA
0131 669 2750
Not Listed
🚌 12, 26, (42), (49)
No food

Foresters Arms

This main-road pub seems to have been refitted shortly before or just after the First World War and is a good place to see an island bar arrangement in the Edinburgh area. The entrance leads into a small lobby, which, no doubt, used to have a jug bar hatch for service. The U-shaped counter has reeded panelling of the same type that lines the walls. The island gantry looks wholly modern. At the rear right is a sitting (now games) room with plainer dado panelling. The lounge to the left is physically separate and currently closed. The Ormelie, 44 Joppa Road in the nearby Joppa area retains its decoratively carved gantry and long bar counter of *c*.1904 and also two of four original snugs.

Old Town

9A Holyrood Road EH8 8AE
0131 556 5044
Category C(s) Listed
🚌 35, 36 and Nicholson Street
   buses
Meals Wed to Fri lunchtimes and
   evenings; Sat & Sun 12 to 7
Real ale

Holyrood Tavern

Bare-boarded pub built in 1898 that retains its original two-tier mirrored gantry. The stand-up bar has an old counter with match-strikers, two-thirds-height wall panelling and an elongated Usher's Pale Ale mirror, but the bar top is new. A wide arch on the right leads to a separate sitting room with more panelling, a few bell-pushes and a 1930s fireplace. There was a snug bar at the front accessed from the left-hand door but only a small section of curved, part-glazed screen that separated it remains. The bar opens out at the rear and there is a good cornice throughout. The pub was extended back in the 1930s, and the rear room is the venue for a folk music jam session on Sunday evenings.

New Town

152–4 Rose Street EH2 3JD
0131 226 1773
Category B Listed
🚊 Waverley
🚌 Princess Street buses
Meals all day
Real ale

Can you tell which tiles on the walls of the Kenilworth, Edinburgh are the original Victorian ones and which date from only 1966? The original tiles (left) have a smooth finish and much of the crazing (crack-like markings on the tiles due to aging) is more like scratches. Where the tiles have a relief/rough finish and the crazing forms a pattern the tiles are the restored/replacement ones (right)

Kenilworth ☆

One of Edinburgh's four impressive 'single-room with island-bar' pubs. The walls are covered in blue and white Minton tiles, topped off with rows of brown and white tiles finishing some two-thirds up the double-height public bar, which has a patterned plasterwork ceiling in red and cream. Built *c*.1780, the Thomas Purves Marwick interior dates from 1899 and was subject to a very costly renovation by Alloa Brewery in 1966 using the architects Covell Matthews. They restored the splendid mahogany island bar to its original position and renovated the decoratively carved front with its brass match-strikers

The Kenilworth, Edinburgh has an impressive almost square island bar counter and ornate gantry. The walls are mostly covered with Minton's tiles.

under the rim; unfortunately, part of the right-hand side was lost in changes prior to 1966. Even the damaged tiles were restored using majolica, and it is difficult to distinguish them from the original Victorian ones. There is a massive Drybrough's of Edinburgh mirror. The short partitioning attached to the bar and the pot shelf are 1966 additions, which is the date the Scott Room, a small lounge/family room, was added to the rear. Note the stained and leaded glass windows on the front and side of the first-floor area.

Newington

45 Ratcliffe Street EH9 1SU
0131 667 7205
Category B Listed
🚌 (42) & Nicholson Street buses
Snacks all day
Real ale

Leslie's Bar ★

A magnificent island-bar pub built in 1899 in a four-storey sandstone tenement by P L Henderson. Similar to the Abbotsford (see page 38), it is well worth going out of your way to visit. It is unique, having a gantry-like structure on the top left-hand side of the bar counter and a series of low, ticket booth-like windows for service, which are numbered on the inside. This arrangement is similar to snob screens seen in Victorian pubs in English cities, which allowed more affluent patrons of the lounge bar to obtain their liquor through low serving hatches and preserve some privacy from public bar customers. This is one of only a handful of pubs selling its own whisky, a fine blended one distilled by Inverarity. On the left as you enter is a snug separated from the lounge by a low, panelled screen with a door and semi-circular stained and leaded glass panels in the top. At the far end of the counter is an elegant mahogany gantry with original Bryson clock and sells.

In the tiny sitting room of Leslie's Bar, Edinburgh, the bar counter has a hinged section which nobody has so far been able to provide an explanation for. Any help on this matter is most welcome.

Other original features include a Lincrusta frieze, an ornate plaster cornice and a highly decorative ceiling picked out in gold paint. The dado panelling is from a neighbouring house and was added during a restoration in 1958. At the rear of the lounge is another snug with a wide doorway, half-height panelled walls and ceiling, also from 1958. In 1971, a former shop was absorbed to become a sitting room, and has a wide doorway. The window screens date from 2005. John Leslie was the second licensee, from 1902 to 1924.

Liberton

88 Kirk Brae EH16 6JA
0131 672 2823
Category C(s) Listed
🚌 7, 31
Snacks all day

Liberton Inn

A three-room pub in a plain, late 19th-/early 20th-century building with a male-dominated, stand-up public bar. The rooms seem to have been mostly refitted in an inter-war scheme with basic, three-quarter-height wall panelling in the public bar on the corner. Formerly two separate rooms until the wall between them was removed in 2006, it retains a 1930s panelled, U-shaped counter, modest island gantry and low window seats. In the small middle lounge, the bar counter appears to be the only survivor from the 1930s, with a gantry and Victorian-style fireplace dating from a late 1980s refit. Carrying on down a passage to the rear and you will find the Reuben Butler lounge, named after the character in Walter Scott's *The Heart of Midlothian*. This two-part lounge, which can also be accessed from Kirkgate, is open only in the evenings and at weekends. The counter and stone fireplace could also be from the 1930s but the gantry is more modern.

Leith

5–7 Restalrig Road EH6 8BB
0131 467 7471
Not Listed
🚌 12, 25
No food

Links Tavern

Although the original counter and gantry at this drinkers' pub were replaced in 1995, there is still much of interest, and the traditional plan, including two snugs, still remains. The gantry is positioned between the two pub entrances, and screens with attractive coloured glass form the two tiny rooms, one of which is now used as an office. Other original features include the fielded panelling around the walls, a fire-surround with pink and green marble and (most of) a St Andrew's cross in tile, and three original William Younger's advertising mirrors.

New Town

1 Queensferry Street EH2 4PA

0131 225 3549

Category B Listed

≋ Haymarket

🚌 Princes Street buses

Snacks all day (not Sun)

Real ale

Only the central three sections of the towering back gantry at H P Mathers are original. The two sections to the left and right were added in the 1960s, but it is not easy to spot the change as the wood carvings are identical to that on the original sections.

H P Mathers ★

This high-ceilinged, male-dominated, single-room pub is little changed in over 100 years. It is located on the ground floor of a five-storey red ashlar building, designed in 1900 by Sydney Mitchell & Wilson for the National Commercial Bank of Scotland and the Caledonian United Services Club. The wine merchant Hugh Mather established the licensed premises in 1902. The porch has colourful floor-to-ceiling tiling. The bar counter is original but has a new top, while the fireplace has new tiles. Other original features include old half-height panelling, a good ceiling and frieze. A ladies toilet with its small screen around the door was relocated from the rear right corner in the 1960s and is now downstairs. The walls are adorned by a number of old brewery mirrors from Edinburgh & Leith Brewery, Mackay's, McEwan's and Wm Younger.

New Town

8 Young Street EH2 4JB

0131 539 7119

Category B Listed

≋ Waverley/Haymarket

🚌 Princes Street buses

Snacks lunchtimes

Real ale

Oxford Bar ★

This small basic pub built in 1811 is the least altered pub in Edinburgh – it is much as it was in the late 19th century. Can you spot those customers and people behind the bar on whom Ian Rankin based his characters in the Inspector Rebus novels? If not, just ask and they will tell you. The tiny stand-up bar in the front left of the pub, with no tables or chairs, and just two sets of bare window seating for about four people set in the dark wood dado panelling on the nicotine-

You could meet Ian Rankin or the people who he based characters in his Inspector Rebus novels on if you pay a visit to the tiny Oxford Bar in Edinburgh.

mustard walls is just as it was. There is an old fireplace on the far left, partly covered up by the bar itself. The pub looks full with a dozen or so customers in it. The mirrored gantry, which has a noticeable slope and some new added shelves, dates from the late 19th century, as does the bar counter, but the bar top is a replacement. Note the old 'Bernard's India Pale Ale' cemented-on lettering on the upper front window – only one letter has been lost. Up three steps and through the doorway on the right is a basic, dimly lit sitting room with shutters on the windows. There is a 1950s brick fireplace and an old 'Murray's Pale Ale' mirror. On the wall of the sitting room is a photo of the bar and former landlord William Ross, who refused to serve women and Englishmen, and anyone ordering a lager would be instantly barred!

Abbeyhill
7 Piershill Place/London Road
EH8 7EH
0131 661 4121
Category B Listed
🚌 (4), 5, 26, 44, 44A
Meals all day to 7pm

Porters

Recently reopened, little-altered pub of 1893, with three rooms and floor mosaic at the entrance that tells us this pub used to be called the Piershill Tavern. The main bar has a counter and panelling dating from just before or after the First World War. The gantry was, no doubt, remodelled at the same time but may incorporate earlier columns. There has been some rearrangement at the front with the jug bar (named in window glass) now incorporated into the main space. There is an odd little hatch between the jug bar area and the modernised lounge to the left, which has dado square panelling all around, three bell-pushes and a modern counter. The large sitting room at the rear was added in 1910 and is now a games room. The stained glass in the doors and various panels seems to be a mixture of both old and relatively new.

New Town

37 Rose Street EH2 2NH
0131 226 5402
Category B Listed
⇌ Waverley
🚌 Princes Street buses
Snacks all day

Robertson's 37 Bar

Rose Street is popular for a pub crawl, and this is one of three true heritage pubs along it. It still retains its splendid tall ornately carved gantry and what is believed to be the original bar counter, which has a frontage added in the 1960s but the top has been renewed. Built as a four-storey red sandstone dwelling in the 19th century, the interior by P L Henderson is dated 1898. It is quite possible that the bar was much as it is today, apart from the rear left section where the original toilets were – these are now downstairs. The only other recent change is the removal of some fixed seating on the right c.2000 to create more space.

Dalry

1 Roseburn Terrace EH12 5NG
0131 337 1067
Category C(s) Listed
🚌 12, 26, 31 & First 12, 16, 38, 86
Snacks all day
Real ale

Roseburn Bar

Close to both Scotland's national rugby stadium Murrayfield and Hearts football ground, this pub is very busy on match days. At the foot of an 1880s four-storey, grey stone tenement, the large high-ceilinged public bar is thought to be much as it was, although the original gantry, as the photo in the bar shows, was increased in height in 1990. The old bar counter has two substantial but short partitions with mirrored panels, and rising from them are two columns with decorative capitals. The room has wall panelling, some to full height and five of the eight old etched window panels remain. There are original mirrors from Campbell & Co and Wm Murray's. Off to the right is a small separate Fly Half Bar that retains its original 'Jug Bar' etched glass in the door, but the panelling and seating are modern. Rugby photos etc. adorn the walls. The lounge, with its separate entrance in Roseburn Street, has an old counter and three columns with capitals, but the gantry and fireplace are modern.

Old Town

3 Drummond Street EH8 9TT
0131 557 8495
Category B Listed
⇌ Waverley
🚌 Nicholson Street buses
No food

Rutherford's ★

Two-room pub in a single-storey building of 1899, the interior, which looks as though it has seen better days, is in a real time warp. It is famous as being one of Robert Louis Stevenson's favourite pubs. It was in the hands of the same family from 1958 to 2006 and seems to have been completely refitted shortly after they took over. The most distinctive features in the public bar are the suspended beams forming an open canopy over the counter and the small Formica-topped tables. The lounge has a hatch to the back of the bar with the word 'Service' in c.1960 lettering; an adjacent bell is for attracting attention. No one could argue that the fittings stand comparison with the rich work of the late Victorian or Edwardian pubs or even some of the sleek, sophisticated examples of the 1930s, but the basic nature of most early post-war pub furnishing means it has fallen victim to later change and Rutherford's is a rare example of where it can be seen in a complete scheme. There is some Victorian decorative glass at the front.

Haymarket

1 Haymarket Terrace EH12 5EY
0131 337 7582
Category B Listed
⮂ Haymarket
🚌 2, 3, 3A, (4), 12, 25, 26, 31, 33, 44, 44A
Meals all day
Real ale

Ryrie's Bar

This busy pub with its splendid wooden frontage occupies two buildings, and was redesigned by Robert MacFarlane Cameron in 1906 for Messrs Ryrie and Company, whisky merchants. Entrance doors on the left both have 'Bar' leaded panels in them, suggesting that the single bar space may have been like this for a very long time. The good, spreading gantry with a still-working clock over the centre is unaltered but, sadly, there is an amount of unnecessary clutter on the top, including some false casks. The original bar counter used to curve around on the right but was shortened in 1992 to improve staff access, and some panelling was resited. There are still working water taps on the bar that were replaced in the 1980s, and some attractive coloured glass advertising various drinks. The right-hand building, which has a stone-carved 'Old Haymarket Inn' sign now covered by a 'Ryrie & Co. Estb. 1862' sign, houses a small sitting room popular with diners. Upstairs is a modern lounge with a 'Sitting Room' window.

Old Town

25 Forest Row EH1 2QH
0131 225 2751
Not Listed
🚌 2, 41, (42) and Nicholson Street buses
No food
Real ale

Sandy Bells

Small folk music pub barely altered in 50 years and with live music seven nights a week and also on Saturday and Sunday afternoons. It has an old gantry, bar counter, vestibule entrance and a fireplace covered by seating. It is divided into two rooms by a pedimented arch, which had the wood panel on the counter replaced by a glass one in recent years. The rear room has been extended by absorbing a narrow passage.

Duddingston

43 The Causeway EH15 3QA
0131 661 1020
Category B Listed
🚌 (4), (42), 44, 44A
Meals all day
Real ale

Sheep Heid Inn

Mid 19th-century village inn with three dimly lit rooms that is popular with diners. A fine place for refreshment for anyone walking to the top of nearby Arthur's Seat (251m/823ft). The small panelled bar is just as it was, with an Edwardian semi-circular bar counter with four pilasters and two water taps (not currently working), and the 100-year-old back gantry is topped off with two mirrors declaring 'Younger of Alloa the

Best Beer Around'. To the left is a small room with dado panelling and an old fireplace; a third room has been brought into use in recent times. An upstairs dining room with modern bar fittings is open weekends only.

At the rear of the Sheep Heid Inn, Duddingston is a popular double lane skittle alley, one of very few in Scotland

Canonmills
2 Broughton Road EH7 4EB
0131 556 2911
Not Listed
🚌 8, 23, 27
No food

Stag's Head

A little-altered Edwardian pub at the foot of a tenement built in 1856. It retains an ornately carved modest gantry, an old bar counter and dado panelling. Until the 1980s, it had a separate jug bar on the right, complete with a hatch, but this is now a small separate area up a couple of steps. Other original features include 'The Stags Head' in mosaic in the doorway, three old whisky mirrors, good ceiling roses and cornices.

Abbeyhill
21 Cadzow Place, London Road
EH7 5SN
0131 661 1020
Not Listed
🚌 1, (4), 5, 19, 26, 34, 36, 44, 44A
No food

The rare intact jug bar.

Station Bar

Virtually unaltered in over 40 years and still with its jug bar, this is a basic working man's pub, which opens at 9am Monday to Saturday. Situated at the bottom of a four-storey tenement building. The public bar retains its original four-bay gantry from the late 1890s and original counter with a heating rail around the base. There is extensive wall panelling, and on the left wall a massive 'Drybrough's Pale & Mild Ales' mirror, which is protected with cardboard for Hibernian home football matches when the pub gets packed. The tiny jug and bottle compartment on the right, created by a low glazed partition with a hatch for service and small shelf, is a tremendous survival. Where the bar counter ends, there is an arch and the public bar opens out, but all the evidence points to the existing layout having always been like this since operating as a pub. At the rear is the small Safari Lounge, which was refitted in the 1960s, complete with bar counter, gantry and ply-panelled walls. However, this is about to be lost when new toilets are installed, the old toilets removed and the drinking area extended to the rear. Across the road, the Artisan, 35 London Road, has a unique 'Maclennan & Urquhart's Celebrated Pale Ale' mirror, which is shaped into the corner under a flight of stairs. This pub is of the island-bar style, with a modern gantry and counter.

New Town
3 Waterloo Place EH1 3BG
0131 556 7597
Category A Listed
🚆 Waverley
🚌 Princes Street buses
Snacks all day

Waterloo Buffet

A tiny high-ceilinged bar that retains its original 100-year-old gantry. It is situated in a three-storey stone building of 1818 designed by Archibald Elliot and is identical to the one across the road. The back gantry, possibly of elm, has high pedimented sections at each end and an arched one in the middle. Two large but relatively new mirrors and very decorative cornice work grace the small room. The bar counter was replaced 30 years ago with a shorter one to accommodate the new ladies toilet; the majority of the panelling is new. On the first floor is the Trafalgar Suite, a long thin room that is currently open only for functions but this may change soon. It has a genuinely old highly decorative bar counter, which is likely to have been imported, with a new polished stone top, but the gantry with bevelled mirror panels dates from a refit in the 1970s. Closes at 10pm Sundays to Thursdays.

FALKIRK

Bo'ness
42–54 North Street EH51 0AG
01506 824717
Category C(s) Listed
No food

Anchor Tavern

This small town pub of 1891, with a basic bar and separate snug, retains its original back gantry incorporating both an 'Usher's India Pale Ale' and a 'Taylor's & Ferguson Scotch Whisky' mirror. As you enter, there is a short partition affixed to the wall with an iron stay. The bar counter is original but with some *c.*1960s facing. All the walls are panelled, there are two good stained and leaded window screens, a 'Hutchinson's Arrow Blend Whisky' mirror and, while not of special note, a geometric-patterned ceiling that adds to the atmosphere. The snug on the left with one rounded end has 1960s ply-panelled walls, leatherette fixed seating and one of two original windows.

Falkirk
150 Grahams Road FK2 7BY
01324 633303
Not Listed
⚥ Grahamston
No food

Star

This 1930s Art Deco drinkers' pub is well worth a visit to see what may be the only glass bar counter in the country, made up of some 160 ribbed glass segments and with a wooden top. The 1930s fittings include a good set of front windows and diagonal door handles. The back gantry has a base, which could date from the 1930s, with a series of drawers, and a top part of sunken shelving with some glass shelves added in the late 1950s. The walls have full-height panelling; there is a 1950s brick fireplace in the opened-up area on the right, and all the fixed seating looks of a similar age. A door from Gowan Street leads into a passage that has an intact off-sales hatch with two sliding windows. In the gents toilet, there was a working penny in the slot on the door until recently but this now resides on the wall of the refurbished lounge upstairs, which has a post-war bar counter, new bar top and new shelves for a gantry.

The quirky, and possibly unique, bar counter made up of 160 glass blocks at the Star, Falkirk

Falkirk

76 High Station Road FK1 5QX
01324 629393
Not Listed
⇌ Falkirk High
No food

Woodside Inn

A popular stand-up drinkers' pub built in 1898 with a U-shaped
original counter that takes up an incredible amount of space
compared to the size of the room. The vestibule entrance has doors
with colourful 'Bar' windows to the left and right, but nowadays you
enter via the half-doors with 'Family Bar' panels in front of you. In the
late 1980s, the two partition walls that formed the off-sales were
removed to create a completely walk-around bar. The panelled walls
are original, as are the Victorian tiled fireplace and the bench seating
opposite, but the island gantry was replaced in 2003 and other seating
renewed. Other original features include a large frieze of fleur-de-lys
and thistles all around the room, two large Geo. Younger's mirrors,
and another for Highland Queen whisky. Carrying on through a wood-
lined arch, the panelled passage has another large Highland Queen
whisky mirror. Further on is the refurbished lounge at the rear with
original panelling and a genuine Victorian fireplace, but this was
imported in the late 1980s. There are also two of the finest surviving
stained and leaded window screens in Scotland – one for Campbell
Hope & King Ales and another for James Brown Wines and Spirits.

FIFE

Earlsferry

5 Links Road KY9 1AW
01333 330610
Not Listed
Meals evenings
Real ale

Golf Tavern (19th Hole)

A recent model refurbishment has not spoiled the public bar that has
barely changed in 100 years, with mirrored back gantry and original
bar counter that was slightly moved in 2005 and is now on a plinth.
Dating from 1836, the pub has full-height panelled walls recently
painted an attractive red, a sanded and varnished wood floor and two

The recently restored public bar
of the Golf Tavern (19th Hole),
Earlsferry

large mirrors of note: one for Haig whisky, the other for Wilson's mineral waters. A partition on the left, which created a separate saloon bar, has been removed and there is a dining room at the rear left that retains its old panelling. At the rear on the right, a small pool room was added in 2005, with wood-panelled walls and ceiling in keeping with the rest of the pub. Closed Mondays in winter.

Kincardine
16 Forth Street FK10 4LX
No phone
Not Listed
No food

Railway Tavern (Scotland's) ★

An amazing survivor: 200 years ago, this tucked-away terrace pub (clearly under a different name) served drovers bringing their livestock south. It would have presented much the same plain appearance as it does today, as the only sign that this is a pub at all are the words

Can you work out which is the entrance to the Railway Tavern, Kincardine? The only indication is the words above the door. Once inside you will find one of the smallest public bars in the whole of Scotland.

above the door: 'J Dobie Licensee'. The Dobie family – the present owner and publican is Ronnie - is said to be the longest-serving family licensees in Fife. Inside is one of the smallest public bars in Scotland, and two other rooms, just one of which is in regular use. Enter down a passage with a partitioned wall, hatch, shelf for passageway drinking and working bell-box. The door on the left leads to the tiny public bar, where there is a bar counter at least 60 years old with a Bakelite top. The back gantry consists of homemade domestic shelves of miscellaneous provenance, and there is a small 1930s cast-iron fireplace with Art Deco detailing. Seating consists of four double seats originally constructed by Alexander's bus builders of Falkirk; there is just one oblong table with well-worn Formica top and cast-iron base. The front right small room with '2' on the door has a decorative pink cast-iron fireplace from the 1930s, half-height panelling, a five-legged table and you can press the bell for table service. The rear left room with '3' on the door contains a decoratively carved antique table and another working bell-push. The fourth small room at the rear with '1' on the door is now used as a storeroom. Open in the evenings from 6.30pm and Saturday lunchtimes.

Kirkcaldy

28 Bogies Wynd KY1 2PH
01592 269056
Category C(s) Listed
≉ Kirkcaldy
Meals lunchtimes and also
    Thu to Sun evenings
Real ale

Two small tiled paintings at the
Feuars Arms, Kirkcaldy.

Feuars Arms ☆

A splendid example of Edwardian pub fitting and especially notable for the display of ceramics, one of the best in Scotland, including an 18m (59ft) long bar counter completely fronted with brown Art Nouveau tiles. The pub was rebuilt in 1890 and then remodelled in 1902 by William Williamson, with two-tone tiled walls, including two small Doulton's of Lambeth tiled panels (each a single tile) featuring a jester evidently eyeing up the shepherdess a few feet away. The large bar has an all-over mosaic floor, a solid mahogany gantry with semi-

The rare glass panelled cistern in the gents' at the Feuars Arms, Kirkcaldy.

octagonal office within, and a long-case clock. Other original features include the stained and leaded windows with the arms of Scotland, England and Ireland, lots of etched glass and two porch floors with mosaic floors, one now opened up. There is a restaurant at the rear left with a hatch but this area has undergone recent changes. Visit the intact gents, if you can, for its glass-panelled Doulton's cistern, pair of marble-framed urinals, tiled walls and mosaic floor. The central entrance on Bogie's Wynd must have led originally to a small off-sales compartment divided from the bars on either side by screens.

Kirkcaldy

471–3 High Street KY1 1JL
01592 264270
Category C(s) Listed
⇌ Kirkcaldy
Snacks all day
Real ale

The jug bar at the Harbour Bar, Kirkcaldy

Harbour Bar

The building dates from c.1870 and was a ship's chandlers until it became a pub in 1924; it is one of few pubs still with a jug bar. In the porch, doors lead to the bar on the right, lounge on the left and in front of you is the tiny intact jug bar with its two half-width doors and two tiny hatches to the bar. The main bar on the right retains its original mirrored back gantry with fluted pilasters, bar counter and half-height panelled walls. At the rear is an area created during a 1960s flat roof extension to the building. The lounge on the left has no old fittings, apart from the panelled ceiling with decorative plasterwork of thistles, roses and clover. Behind the pub is the Fyfe brewery, established in 1995. Closed in the afternoons from Monday to Wednesday inclusive.

Leslie

203 High Street KY6 3AZ
No phone
Category C(s) Listed
No food

Auld Hoose ★

Terraced drinkers' pub built c.1900 that has been in the same family since 1933 and has barely changed. It consists of two L-shaped bars arranged symmetrically either side of a screened off-sales compartment and a snug attached to the counter. Although not visually exciting,

The Auld Hoose, Leslie, has barely changed since the 1920s with two bars, tiny sitting room and off-sales.

the intactness of this pub is very rare. The panelled bar on the far left has a ribbed wood counter, a 1920/30s tiled and wood-surround fireplace, and 1960s fitted seating. Note the old 'Bar' and 'Tennants' cemented-on lettering on the glass. The tiny off-sales on the left of the entrance is a part-glazed wood partitioned room with a tiny hatch to the bar. The snug on the right of the entrance is similar in style to the off-sales and is twice the size with an open counter. The lounge on the far right is very similar to the bar; note the old pressure gauge that is part of the electric air compressor used to dispense beer in the past (see page 77). There are only basic shelves making up the back gantry, which is of no great age. There is a large 'Auld House Luncheon Bar Fine Old Cameron Bridge Whisky' mirror in the panelled passage to the toilets. Closed Wednesday lunchtime.

TRY ALSO   **Coaledge Tavern**, 1 Coaledge, Mossgreen, Crossgate KY4 8BU (Tel: 01383 510027). Close to junction 3 of the M90 is this small village pub that is worth a visit for the 100-year-old semi-circular bar counter. The island gantry is apparently cut down, there are some back gantry shelves, and the pub was last changed in the 1960s, when a small area on the rear right was opened up.

CITY OF GLASGOW

City Centre

17–19 Drury Street G2 5AE

0141 229 5711

Category B Listed

⊖ Buchanan Street/St Enoch

⇌ Central

Meals lunchtimes and evenings

Real ale

Horseshoe Bar ★

One of the finest examples of an island bar open-plan pub in Scotland. It has the longest continuous bar in the UK, measuring 32m (104ft 3in). Built in 1870 and remodelled in 1885–7 by John Scouller and again in 1901, when the partitions between sitting rooms and the bar were removed. The elongated horseshoe-shaped bar counter, which has an old terrazzo spittoon trough all around it, was also extended at the rear. The initials JYW in small etched glazed screens on the bar top refer to John Young Whyte, who succeeded Scouller in 1923. The island gantry includes eight casks on their sides with, unusually, two taps in them; until the 1930s, they were used to dispense spirits, including the house speciality 'Lachie', a ten-year-old blend of Highland malt whiskies. The fine mosaic floor was added during a refurbishment in 1985, when the superb dark-stained matchboard ceiling was covered over and a new skylight added. On the rear wall there are two horseshoe-shaped fireplaces with large 'The Horseshoe' mirrors above each one and a clock with the letters 'The Horseshoe' instead of numbers. The wood-panelled walls with decorative

The Horseshoe Bar, Glasgow has the longest continuous bar in the UK at 104 feet 3 inches in circumference.

strapwork at the top have large bell-pushes, most of which are in attractive panels all around the room. At the front are two good stained and leaded window screens and two large mirrors, one with 'JYW' and the other advertising 'Lachie' whisky. The upstairs lounge with modern fittings is a popular venue for karaoke from 8pm each evening and 4pm on Sundays.

City Centre
58 Bridge Street G5 9HU
0141 429 0869
Not Listed
⊖ Bridge Street
Snacks all day

Laurieston Bar

The exterior, with its tiny patterned tiles and distinctive lettering, prepares us for what is, in its way, one of the most remarkable pub interiors in the UK: a full-blown and now very rare *c.*1960 remodelling of an island bar style. Not surprisingly for a nation just emerging from post-war austerity, pub schemes of that time have none of the class of grandiose Victorian developments or the sleek elegance of the 1930s. However, the design style is unmistakable. The entrance from Bridge Street has a small off-sales facing it. On the left comes the public bar with fixed seating around the walls, a series of small, screwed-down, two-tier Formica tables and contemporary low chairs. The boarded elongated oval bar counter (with Formica top) is a fairly simple affair, not unlike work of the 1930s, but the suspended structure over it and the panelling of the ceiling are quintessentially 1960s. There's even a *c.*1960 heated glass food display unit on the counter that is still in use today for hot pies and bridies. The lounge is a smarter place, carpeted unlike the boarded public bar, with more fixed seating, panelling and a number of bell-pushes for table service. To complete the picture, the Formica-covered walls in both the ladies and gents may not exactly strike you as tasteful but they are as much an historical document as Victorian tiling – only much rarer!

The Laurieston Bar, Glasgow has a rare surviving 1960s remodelling of an older island-style bar.

City Centre

1–3 Paisley Road West G51 1LF
0141 429 3135
Category B Listed
⊖ Shields Road
Snacks all day

Old Toll Bar ★

Glasgow's finest pub interior, situated on the ground floor of a three-storey tenement built in 1860 and remodelled in 1892–3. One hundred years ago, there were many ornate pubs like this throughout the city, as publicans went to great lengths to outshine their competitors at a time when skilled labour was cheap. This is one of the last remaining 'palace pubs' in Glasgow; sadly, similar interiors have been ripped out in recent times only to be replaced by poorer-quality modern fittings. The large bar has a magnificent dark wood back gantry incorporating two sets of four whisky casks either side of a mirrored centrepiece, a pediment and central clock. There was a tier of smaller barrels in the recess below the large casks but they were removed some time ago. The original long bar counter with some part-glazed short partitions has a new polished stone top. On the dark wood-panelled walls are four superb huge advertisement mirrors painted and gilded by Forest and Son of Glasgow, one of the largest suppliers of decorated mirrors in the UK in the 1890s. Note the colourful painted windows on the two sets of inner doors and in the vestibule entrance on Admiral Street, where a jug and bottle was originally situated. Other original features include a panelled ceiling, carved woodwork and mahogany panels above the seating; there are only modern fittings in the downstairs

The Old Toll Bar, Glasgow is one of the last remaining 'palace pubs' in Glasgow.

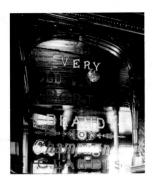

The four large advertising mirrors on the walls of the Old Toll Bar, Glasgow.

lounge bar. Across the road is the Viceroy, a pub little altered in the past 30 years and still with an island bar. It has a couple of colourful glass panels in the doors and, on a Saturday night, table service is still offered to patrons in the rear sitting room.

City Centre
129 St Georges Road G3 6JA
0141 332 5125
Not Listed
⊖ St Georges Cross
⇌ Charing Cross
Snacks should now be available

Oscar Slater's

This dimly lit island-style bar was formerly called the Carnarvon Bar. A sympathetic refurbishment in 2004 has left the layout and fittings much as they have been for many years. It retains the original Edwardian island bar counter, an old island gantry and three snugs, where the panelling was recently repainted and the fixed seating renewed. A fourth snug situated on the front right was lost many years ago and the ladies toilets in the rear right were only added in recent years. Cast-iron pillars support the high-coffered ceiling with good cornice work but the quarry-tiled floor is new.

City Centre
112 Stockwell Street G1 4LW
0141 552 8681
Not Listed
⊖ St Enoch
⇌ Argyll Street
Meals lunchtimes
Real ale

Scotia Bar

First licensed in 1815, this pub is famous for a folk music tradition started in the early 1960s, the most famous artist to appear here being the Glasgow legend Billy Connolly. The mock-Tudor frontage and a number of fittings date from a refurbishment in 1929. The bar counter has the old terrazzo spittoon trough around the base and match-strikers all along the top; there is a mirrored back gantry and a part-glazed partition on the left, which creates a separate small bar. Following a period of closure, the pub was refurbished by Brendan McLaughlin in 1987, which is the date of the rear section of the back gantry, the short partitions and panelled walls. On the right, another partition creates a snug on two levels, and there are signs of another snug at the front where some bell-pushes remains. These days the live music is more varied and you will find musicians performing every Wednesday to Saturday evening and also at 4.30pm on Saturdays and Sundays.

City Centre

62 Glassford Street G64 1LJ

0141 552 3059

Category B Listed

⊖ St Enoch

⇌ Argyll Street/Queen Street

Rolls all day

The hooped stall
on the counter.

Steps Bar ★

This spartan city centre bar is an amazing survivor: refitted in 1938, it has barely altered since. It is one of three impressive 1930s Art Deco survivors in Glasgow – the others being the Portland Arms, also in this guide, and Rogano's an upmarket seafood restaurant and bar. Situated on the ground floor of a late 18th-century four-storey building, the bar has been owned by the same family for 40 years; its name comes from the two steps into the pub. It has an Art Deco frontage of Vitrolite panelling and frosted glass window, one of which was replaced in 2006. The interior is complete with sleek veneer-panelled walls, the original back gantry of Australian walnut, and the original bar counter. The hooped stall on the counter indicates an area for use only by bar staff offering waiter service to the customers in the splendid sitting room at the rear left. This small room also has more sleek veneer-panelled walls, original fixed seating and a stained glass window depicting the Cunard liner *Queen Mary* with a Spitfire flying above. Why not take a seat here and press the bell, as it is still possible to take advantage of the increasingly rare table service? The only changes have been the replacement of floor coverings, the new gents toilets at the rear and the adding of a ladies for the first time in the 1950s.

Steps Bar, Glasgow is an impressive 1930s Art Deco survivor

TRY ALSO

Bastile at Sloans a pub close by which has a vestibule entrance, richly decorated in Victorian tiles, leading from Argyle Arcade. The public bar has lost its original opulent character but Edwardian fittings survive in the upstairs rooms, which are now used mainly for functions.

City Centre

159 Bridgegate G1 5HZ
0141 552 6040
Not Listed
⊖ St Enoch
⇌ Argyll Street
No food
Real ale

Victoria Bar

The 'Vicky Bar' is an old-fashioned, dimly lit Victorian public bar with full-height dark-stained matchboard walls and a ceiling held up by cast-iron pillars. The panelling was exposed only recently, having been covered by plasterboard and wallpaper for some years. The back gantry is adorned with a mirror advertising Robert Younger's extinct St Ann's brewery; it may have come from another pub but has been here many years. Other features of note are the original counter with match-strikers all along it and, as you enter, part-glazed partitions that create a snug on the left. The lounge, added just after the Second World War, is a conversion from a former fishmonger's shop. Occasional live music.

Pollockshields

708 Pollokshaws Road G41 2AD
0141 423 0380
Not Listed
⇌ Pollockshields West/
   Queens Park
🚌 45, 57, (12, 66)
No food

Heraghty's Bar

Small Edwardian drinkers' pub with an elegant carved back gantry that is adorned with mirrors, columns and decorative capitals. The bar counter, which has modern tiles around the base, was installed in the 1930s, which is the date of the Art Deco stained glass. Other original fittings include a large column in the middle of the room, with a number of now redundant match-strikers, a modest frieze and old wall panelling. The fixed seating looks at least 30 years old, while the ladies toilet was only installed in 1996 following complaints!

Shettleston

1169 Shettleston Road G32 7NB
0141 778 6657
Category B Listed
⇌ Shettleston
🚌 40, 62
No food

Portland Arms ★

This, the most intact of Glasgow's unspoilt pubs, has an island bar interior in a 'streamlined' Art Deco style. It is a popular drinkers' pub that gets packed when Celtic are playing. A single-storey brick building with a polished stone frontage is still owned by the same family since it

An amazing Art Deco survivor –
the interior of the Portland Arms,
Shettleston.

was rebuilt in 1938 by Thomas Sandilands & Macleod. This remarkable
survivor has a splendid oval bar counter with a 'zebra-like' veneer
panelling and match-strikers all around the metal rim. The original
island gantry has a lighting canopy above it. All the walls are veneer-
panelled; there are Art Deco fireplaces on the left- and right-hand sides,
and original fixed seating with wooden dividers and match-strikers
on them. In front of the entrance door is the small unchanged 'Family
Dept.' (jug and bottle) with its small hatch to the bar. On the left at
the front is a small office now used as a cleaners' store. In each of the
four corners of the pub are small sitting rooms, the front ones with
part-glazed partition walls and the one on the right labelled 'Ladies
Room'. These all have veneer-panelled walls, fixed seating around
just one table and bell-pushes. The only changes since 1938 are the
replacement of the original geometric-patterned floor covering and
modernisation of the toilets.

Shettleston

1410–16 Shettleston Road
G32 9AL
0141 778 2368
Not Listed
⇌ Shettleston
🚌 40, 62
No food

Railway Tavern ★

An old single-storey pub with possibly the most intact Glasgow-style
island bar interior. It has one of the few remaining family departments
(off-sales) in the city and two small sitting rooms. The left-hand door
has a vestibule entrance with doors to the left and right, where a
partition creates a separate bar at the front of the pub. The original
carved island gantry still has two old till drawers, one of which retains
the small lead containers for coins. The original island counter has a
Formica top placed over the original. The right-hand exterior door
leads into the intact family department, formed by two part-glazed
partitions. The only other way to enter this tiny room is via the very
rare 90cm- (3ft-) high door at the rear of the bar, originally used by

cleaning staff to access the room without going outside. The dado is panelled throughout, and there are two tiled fireplaces in the bar area and another in the front sitting room, which are difficult to date – they are either just pre- or post-war. The sitting rooms with numbers '2' and '3' above them have old bell-pushes, and there are no signs that the rooms ever had doors. The inside toilets were added in the 1950s and, as the old bell-box on the wall with three windows indicates, there was almost certainly a third sitting room, which is where the ladies now is. The floor throughout is probably a piece of 1960s work made up of small tile pieces. The original Art Nouveau etched windows have been replaced.

The partitioned Railway Tavern, Shettleston has the most intact Glasgow-style island bar interior, which dates from c.1905.

Inverness
108–10 Academy Street
IV1 1LX
01463 245990
Category B Listed
⇌ Inverness
Meals lunchtimes and evenings
(not Sun)
Real ale

The island bar at the Phoenix, Inverness.

Phoenix

Built in 1894, the spartan public bar is of classic Scottish island bar-style. It is much as it was, with the original island counter, a terrazzo former spittoon trough running all the way around the base and three disused Dalex tall fonts. However, the island gantry was replaced in 1983. The shallow vestibule has curved, etched side windows and 'Push' on the inner door panels. The floor pattern could indicate a partition that divided the drinking space in two. The water engine (see page 77) used to raise the beer from the cellar has been converted to electric power and can be seen in an illuminated case high up on the rear wall of the bar. In the 1980s, the pub expanded into the property on the right and, apart from a ceiling rose, the lounge, 'Morgan's', has no old fittings.

Rosemarkie
48 High Street IV10 8UF
01381 620164
Category C(s) Listed
Meals lunchtimes and evenings
Real ale

Plough

Village pub rebuilt in 1907 that retains its small public bar almost intact. This has an original semi-circular counter and back gantry holding a number of single malt whiskies. The room is completely wood-panelled, with a tongue-and-groove ceiling. The stone lintel over the fireplace with a date of 1691 is all that remains from the original building of that date. The fireplace

could be a 1950s replacement but the 'Dewar's Perth Whisky' mirror above is at least as old as the pub. Inner doors have pictorial etched panels but the tiled floor is new. Behind the bar the tiny gents toilet consists of only one small urinal. At the rear are a lounge and, beyond that, a dining room both with new fittings.

INVERCLYDE

Gourock
64–5 Shore Street PA19 1RF
01475 632042
Not Listed
⇌ Gourock
No food

Monteiths

Small drinkers' pub built in the 1890s that retains its original seven-tier back gantry and U-shaped bar counter. The public bar has good cornice work and two old mirrors, but the panelling and seating areas date from the 1990s. The rear sitting room with '2' on the door has some fixed seating, which is possibly inter-war. Originally, the left-hand door led to a ladies' snug but the partition was removed some years ago – its position was where the old terrazzo spittoon trough around the base of the bar finishes. Look for the stuck-on lettering high up on the right-hand porch advertising 'Campbell's Edinburgh Ales' and various spirits.

Gourock
1 Hopeton Street/
105 Shore Street PA19 1PG
01475 633152
Category B Listed
Snacks all day; restaurant Tues
   to Sat lunchtimes and
   evenings, Sun lunchtimes

Victoria Bar

This local institution has a stand-up bar for drinkers and a popular modernised lounge on the left. In a 19th-century building, it has an island style bar of *c.*1900. A porch on the right-hand side has three doors, two of which lead to the terrazzo-floor bar; the other was for the off-sales but this now leads to a service area. The original counter has an old spittoon trough around the base, and the gantry was replaced in 1993, although it is a true replica of the original. The lounge on the left was opened up in 1990 and extended back, and there is a restaurant on the first floor with a separate entrance. There are very few optics, with most spirits served from the bottle into measures. The pub was owned by the McMillan family for 50 years until 1987 and has always been closed on Sundays. Despite the change in the law in 1976 that allowed pubs in Scotland to open on a Sunday for the first time, the family never applied for a licence. New owner Ron Pollock has continued this tradition, although the restaurant does open for Sunday lunches.

Greenock
7 Laird Street PA15 1LB
01475 720028
Not Listed
⇌ Greenock
No food

Black Cat

Town centre locals' pub of classic island bar-style with only a narrow area around it for drinkers. Apart from repainting, it has remained much as it is today for over 50 years. It retains an island counter at least 70 years old, with a replacement top, and a modest island gantry. The porch has a terrazzo floor, which is also the material used for the old spittoon trough around the bar. There is a good cornice, and the whole room has old dado panelling. The only significant change in the past 50 years is the adding of a ladies toilet. Popular with Celtic fans.

Gothenburg Pubs

COLIN VALENTINE

In the late 19th and early 20th century, a style of pub became popular in the mining areas of the Lothians and Fife, known as Gothenburgs. This system of pub management started in 1865 in Gothenburg, Sweden, in a bid to stem the rising tide of drunkenness. Laws were passed granting all public house licences to a trust charged with running the pubs, and managers had no incentive to promote alcohol sales but could benefit from food and non-alcoholic drinks sales. Profits above 5% of capital employed went back to the municipal treasury.

While there are still pubs in Lowland Scotland called The Goth or Gothenburg, very few of them still operate as Gothenburgs. However, the Dean Tavern in Newtongrange, just south of Edinburgh, still operates on Gothenburg lines, as does the Goth in Armadale, West Lothian. These have been joined by the Prestoungrange Gothenburg at Prestonpans, which was meticulously restored and re-opened in 2003.

This pub, the **Prestoungrange Gothenburg** at Prestonpans, and the Dean Tavern at Newtongrange are run in a different way from all the other pubs in this guide.

So what is a Gothenburg? These pubs are community, or co-operative, pubs in the true sense of the word, in that they are owned and run by a board of trustees in a similar way to a committee running a members club. At Newtongrange, all the profits are ploughed back into the pub or paid out in disbursements to the community. The local bowling green and cricket pitch with pavilion were built with money from the Dean Tavern and Newtongrange Gala day, and the silver band and pipe band are still beneficiaries. At Prestoungrange, after a 5% pa cumulative return on the capital employed in the enterprise, all further surpluses are Gift Aid granted to the Prestoungrange Arts Festival, which is a charity devoting all its resources to using the arts to stimulate and encourage the economy of Prestonpans and its vicinity. At Armadale, the community trust can make grants from £30 to an occasional £200–300.

The other working **Goth** in Armadale, West Lothian, which had a clock tower added in 1924. Some pubs used the name of the company formed to run them, hence the quirky name of this former Gothenburg run pub in Fallin, near Stirling.

Port Glasgow
12 Bay Street PA14 5ED
01475 741146
Not Listed
≥ Port Glasgow
No food

Prince of Wales

A town centre drinking man's bar of large island bar-style situated at the foot of a four-storey sandstone tenement. A large vestibule entrance has doors to the left and right leading into the large public bar, with four pillars holding up the ceiling. The third door led to the tiny family bar, which has lost one of its partition walls. The oval-shaped counter took up as much space as the customer's area so, in 1985, the rear curved section was chopped off and a new piece of bar counter added to increase the drinking space. The modest old gantry is attached to one of the pillars and there are a number of post-war seating areas around the room. Other old fittings include the dado-panelled walls, the numbers on the doors, including a '4' on the cellar, and a brick floor around the room abutting the walls.

MIDLOTHIAN

Newtongrange
80 Main Street EH22 8NA
0131 663 2419
Category C(s) Listed
🚌 Lothian 3, 3A, 29 and
　　First 95, X95
Meals Mon to Thur lunchtimes;
　　Fri and Sat all day; Sun
　　12.30–6

Dean Tavern

One of only three pubs in Scotland still operating along Gothenburg lines (see page 70). This multi-roomed pub with a massive public bar has been carefully modernised over the years. It was rebuilt in 1910. The public bar has three arched pillars supporting the roof in the centre of the room, so it looks like two high-ceilinged rooms with a U-shaped counter protruding from the left-hand wall. In 1962, the Dean was extended, and a games room, lounge bar, function room and wine store added. A new back gantry was also added at the rear left, while a

new top and facing were given to the original bar counter. In a further refurbishment in 1997, panelling replaced the original green-tiled walls, the gantry within the U was replaced, minor changes were made to the back gantry, and the function room was modernised. Although the jug bar has been lost, two open snugs still remain. Recently, a sitting room on the left was converted to a restaurant, and the wine store that operated until 2005 is now the kitchen. Upstairs, the former Temperance Bar is now used as a meeting room. It has some old fittings, including a disused Art Deco bar with hatch. In 1962, the Dean became the first pub in Scotland to have beer delivered in tanks.

MORAY

Craigellachie
On A95 towards Keith
AB38 9RR
01340 881239
Not Listed
No food

Fiddichside Inn ★

A marvellous rural survival: a tiny bar at the end of a cottage in a beautiful spot by a bridge over the River Fiddich. The owners are in their 70s/80s, and the pub has been in the same family for 88 years. The public bar measures about 3×4.5 m (10×15ft), with an original panelled counter running down the length of the room and leaving only half of the space for customers. There is not enough room for any tables, only bar stools and a couple of benches. The back gantry is a simple three-bay affair, and there is half-height wooden panelling on the walls. Opposite the counter is a coal fire, and there are antique William Younger's and Robert Younger's IPA mirrors. That's it – no carpets, no food, no fruit machines, no piped music, no TV, no children – absolute heaven for lovers of unspoilt pubs. Open lunchtimes and evenings Monday to Friday, and all day Saturday and Sunday.

The tiny bar at the Fiddichside Inn, Craigellachie.

NORTH AYRSHIRE

Dalry
28 Main Street KA24 5DH
01294 832394
Cateogry C(s) Listed
⇌ Dalry
No food

Volunteer Arms

A drinkers' pub built in 1870 that has never sold spirits via optics – all are served from the bottle into measures. It has been in the same family for 100 years and is practically unchanged since refits in 1958 and 1960, when a snug at the rear of the bar was removed. Although not visually exciting, the counter and back gantry are those installed in 1958 and are rare survivors. On the left-hand side of the public bar there are two sitting rooms created by wooden partition walls and separated by a passage from the side door. Each snug has a sliding door from the passage, leatherette fixed seating and bell-pushes. At the rear is an intact lounge, created in 1960 from former private accommodation. The lounge has a bar counter, mirrored gantry, fixed seating, two tiled and timber-edged fireplaces, all of 1960s vintage.

NORTH LANARKSHIRE

Shotts
82 Shottskirk Road ML7 4EP
01501 822416
Not Listed
⇌ Shotts
No food

Old Wine Store

This edge-of-town pub with a stand up drinkers' bar is possibly the only one in Scotland still selling whisky from the barrel. Situated in a building dated 1927, it has a U-shaped bar counter and island gantry, which are believed to have come from the original Old Wine Store pub situated 100 yards up the road. Note the tiny 'Doctor's Special' mirror on the lower end of the gantry and the small till drawer. The pub still retains a working off-sales on the left but the partition that separates it from the bar has been replaced in recent years. On the right side of the room there are some new low partitions and fixed seating. Until 2003, this area consisted of three snugs. The games room at the rear is a conversion of a former ground-floor cellar. The ladies toilet was added in the 1970s.

The fine spirit cask gantry at the Old Wine Store, Shotts, where the third one on the left is still in use and dispenses a Whyte & McKay's blended whisky.

Wishaw

121 Main Street ML2 7AU
01698 372320
Not Listed
⇌ Wishaw
Food: Ring to check

Imperial Bar

This town centre drinkers' pub is most interesting for its layout, with a series of snugs on the side and another small snug at the front, which was once the preserve of ladies. Most of the fittings you see today were probably installed a decade or so after the Second World War, as they have a flimsiness not usually associated with inter-war work. Along the left-hand side, the four booths have high sides, and three of them are just large enough to accommodate a table and seats around three sides. The back gantry, which is modern, and bar counter are arranged on the right-hand side, parallel to the snugs. The ladies' snug (locked but viewable on request) has seats and a glazed screen with a hatch on the counter. Even though ladies are now allowed access to the main part of the pub, they still do not have the benefit of toilets of their own (but use the gents by timing things right!). A large rear lounge has been added quite recently.

PERTH & KINROSS

Blairgowrie

101 Perth Street PH10 6DT
01250 873142
Not Listed
No food
Real ale

Stormont Arms

A little-altered drinkers' pub that stocks its own label 25-year-old blended whisky with a cask strength of 59%. The public bar has a 100-year-old gantry, an old bar counter with a replacement front, and two old mirrors – one for Dewar's whisky, the other for Bell's. The off-sales and its sliding hatch have been retained. The lounge has some fittings from the 1950s, and there is another room in a small extension with old fixed seating but the fireplaces have been lost. Unaltered gents. Opens at 2pm Tuesday to Thursday.

Harrietfield

Up a short lane by the telephone box, just off B8063 PH1 3DT
01738 880242
Not Listed
No food
Real ale

Drumtochty Tavern

Very rural, early 19th-century comfortable village pub with a small bowling green that is much as it was in the early 1960s. The small public bar retains an old gantry with drawers and four whisky mirrors. The bar counter was replaced in the 1960s, as were the fixed seating and brick fireplace, but the panelled walls are old. Markings on the floor show that the area behind the bar was originally greater than that for drinkers. The games room on the left has a small bar counter, back gantry and fireplace from the 1960s. On the right are two small rooms brought into use in recent years. The first, which is the venue for musicians on the first Tuesday in the month, has a 'John Wright & Co's India Pale Ale' mirror. Has an outside gents. Closed Tuesday lunchtimes.

RENFREWSHIRE

Paisley

7 New Street PA1 1XU
0141 849 0472
Category A Listed
⇌ Paisley Gilmour Street
🚌 First 9 to/from Glasgow
Meals lunchtimes (not Sun)
Real ale

Art Nouveau detail on the bar
at the Bull, Paisley.

Bull Inn ★

Superbly preserved town centre pub, with a great deal of its original
Art Nouveau interior intact, which can get very busy at weekends.
It retains a spirit cask gantry and six sets of four spirit cocks (the only
ones we are aware of in Scotland), which were used originally to
dispense whisky and other spirits from the casks. This four-storey, red
sandstone ashlar tenement building, complete with a conical-roofed
turret, was built in 1901 by W D McLennan. Beyond the stained and
leaded front windows is a dark wood-panelled public bar with an
impressive back gantry running down the right-hand side and
containing four, large, elongated, upright whisky barrels and four
smaller spirit casks. Over the original long bar counter are six arched
service areas – an unusual survival. On the left-hand side of the room
is a splendid terrazzo-tiled and wood-surround fireplace with a
mirrored overmantel, which rises some 3.7m (12ft) up the wall,
and two old fixed seating areas with timber and leaded glass short
partitions. Moving on to the back of the pub, you will find a timber and
leaded glass partition; beyond it there are three snugs, one of which
still retains its door. The book *People's Palaces* has a plan showing that
there were four snugs originally – two on the left and two at the rear.
New toilets have replaced the rear snugs, which explains why the
ladies has a '3' on the door and the gents, a '4'. The snug on the right
was originally a private room. Each snug has an old fireplace, some
have bell-pushes, but the seating has been replaced and the leaded
glass windows are modern.

Paisley

18 Moss Street PA1 1BL
0141 889 2742
Not Listed
≥ Paisley Gilmour Street
🚌 First 9 to/from Glasgow
Snacks Mon to Fri lunchtimes

Lang's Bar

Town centre pub refitted in the 1930s and little altered with a stand-up bar. It retains its original island bar counter, island gantry and has, down both sides of the pub, two impressive large 1930s brick fireplaces. The only significant alteration was the opening-up of the rear sitting room by the removal of a wall in the early 1990s, when the island counter was extended back, as indicated by the old terrazzo spittoon trough around the base, which finishes abruptly. In the rear section is another 1930s brick fireplace, but the dado panelling and fixed seating are new. Both gents toilets are little altered with terrazzo floors. The tiny snug between the two front doors was originally Mr Lang's office.

One of two amazing brick fireplaces at Lang's Bar, Paisley

SCOTTISH BORDERS

Ancrum

The Green (on B6400)
TD8 6XH
01835 830344
Category C(s) Listed
Meals lunchtimes and evenings
Real ale

Cross Keys

Village pub built *c*.1850 of red sandstone and retaining much of its 1906 refurbishment by Jedburgh Brewery. The passage through the pub has 'Bar' etched on panels in the inner doors and a hatch, which was originally for off-sales. The small public bar on the right with a sliding door retains its Edwardian interior fittings of back gantry, counter (the bar top is new) and tiled fireplace. The fixed seating is probably 40 years old. Beyond this is a small dado-panelled room with an original fireplace and mirrored overmantel, but the bar counter and fixed seating are modern additions. The two rear rooms have been brought into use and the only item of interest is the overhead 'tram lines' used for moving heavy casks. This room was the original cellar, where beer was delivered in either a cask called 'a barrel', which contained 36 gallons, or in a hogshead containing 54 gallons. Nowadays, real ale is supplied in either a 9-gallon container called a firkin, or an 18-gallon one called a kil (short for kilderkin). Open lunchtimes (not Monday), Monday to Friday evenings and all day Saturday and Sunday.

Tall Founts

The Traditional Scottish Cask-Beer Dispense Method

Scotland has its own unique method for dispensing cask-conditioned beer (real ale): the tall fount (the 'u' is silent), through which the beer is raised by air pressure using a water engine (hydraulic pressure engine). Introduced in the 1870s, the fount requires air pressures ranging from 12lb psi to as much as 40lb psi, depending upon the available mains pressure. The tap is opened and beer is served at the counter by 'pushing' the beer by air pressure, as compared to the English method of drawing it by suction using a beer-engine (hand-pump). It is an efficient way to produce a pint of real ale in prime condition, with an enticing, naturally produced creamy head. This once-common method of serving beer is, however, rarely used now but various founts are still to be found on Scottish bar counters. They include the Albany, invented by John McGlashan (1876), the Allan & Bogle (1885), Laidlaw (1935), Gaskell & Chambers Dalex (1946) and the Aitken Mk 1 (1962) to Mk 3 (1980s). As these traditional Scottish founts are tall, have a tap at the top and look remarkably like the lager and keg fonts we see today, they have been replaced by the handpump as the widely perceived correct method of serving real ale.

Albany is one of three manufacturers of water engines and thought by many to be the most efficient. The old air pressure gauge can still be seen at Auld House in Leslie and the Crown in Arbroath. In pubs still

using the tall fount, the water engines have been replaced by electric air compressors.

Where to see founts in use today

There are over 50 pubs in this guide serving real ale, the vast majority by handpumps, but only three still use founts, and they are all in Edinburgh. The Abbotsford, Athletic Arms (Diggers) and Wee Bennet's all use Aitken's founts. The Athletic Arms has always served cask McEwan's 80/- from tall founts by air pressure, which is nowadays generated by two electric air compressors. In addition, Bow Bar and Thomson's Bar, two authentic-looking re-creations of Scottish bars, both in Edinburgh, use Aitken founts.

The **Abbotsford**, Edinburgh serves all its cask beers using Aitken founts.

Above middle: The Albany water engine at the Golf Tavern, Bishopton, a pub due to be included in this guide but, at the time of going to press, it was closed and up for sale.

CAMRA is grateful to Duncan McAra for his help in compiling this article and providing the diagram of the founts.

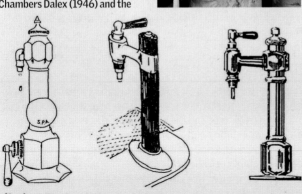

(l-r): McGlashan 'Albany'; Gaskell & Chambers 'Dalex'; Aitken

Coldstream
75–7 High Street TD12 4AE
01890 882391
Not Listed
Meals lunchtimes and evenings
Real ale

Besom Inn

Three-roomed town centre pub with a little-altered Edwardian bar and a room dedicated to the Coldstream Guards. Built in the 1890s and revamped *c*.1910, the public bar retains its original bar counter and gantry, 1950s dado panelling and original glass panel etched with 'Bar' in the door. The lounge has 'Smoke Room' etched in the panel of its door. The hatch was replaced by a small bar counter *c*.1990. The pub was extended to the rear in 1954, and through the wooden archway is a room with full-height panelling, bell-pushes and Coldstream Guards memorabilia, including a visitors' book. The pool room on the right has been brought into use recently.

Galashiels
22 High Street TD1 1SE
01896 753520
Category C(s) Listed
🚌 62, 62A, 62B, 95, X95
Meals lunchtimes

Harrow

Town centre pub built in 1868, refitted *c*.1900, still with its splendid island bar counter with canopy running all the way around. The counter retains old match-strikers and water taps, although they are no longer in use; the pot shelf is modern. The small island gantry could be over 30 years old, and there are remains of two old fireplaces in this large panelled room. The public bar has been opened up towards the rear on the right.

Hawick
11 Green Terrace TD9 0JG
01450 377469
Not Listed
🚌 95, X95
No food

High Level Bar

A *c*.1900 terraced drinkers' pub with a splendid unaltered public bar. It retains the original semi-circle bar counter, two-part mirrored back gantry, half-height panelling, but the fixed seating has been replaced. Note the old bell-box opposite the counter. The jug bar has seen some changes but retains its hatch and an etched door panel has been resited. The modernised lounge on the right has an old panel in the door etched with 'Sitting Rooms', indicating it was formerly two small rooms.

Hawick
32 High Street /4 Cross Wynd
TD9 9EG
01450 372057
Category C(s) Listed
🚌 95, X95
No food

Queens Head

Built in 1895 as a hotel, this is now a basic town centre drinkers' pub with a rare partitioned sitting room. The bar retains both its original counter with water taps and the lower part of the back gantry; the highly decorative upper part was imported *c*.1970 but is undoubtedly older. This high-ceilinged, dado-panelled room has decorative cornice work and a number of ceiling roses. Good set of window screens, including McEwan's. As this guide went to press, the pub closed and is up for sale, so upon reopening there may be changes.

Jedburgh

52 High Street TD8 6DQ
01835 862237
Not Listed
No food

Railway Tavern

Although lacking fittings of quality, this small, three-roomed basic locals' boozer is a throwback to the early 1960s. A sliding door leads into the bar on the right with a Formica-fronted counter (the top was replaced in the early 1980s) and simple mirror back gantry with Formica shelves below. There is a small 1930s cast-iron fireplace with Art Deco detailing, a dado of ply panelling and leatherette-covered wall benches. There is a little-used, tiny, ply-panelled lounge with leatherette seating on the left. An upstairs bar has a counter installed in 1980s, replacing a hatch. The brick fireplace, leatherette seating and tables all date from the early 1960s.

Kelso

Crawford Street TD5 7DP
01573 224817
Not Listed
No food

Red Lion Inn

Situated just off the market place, this multi-roomed pub built in 1905 has been greatly modernised, with the rear rooms popular with young people. However, the public bar retains its original fittings virtually unaltered. There is a splendid back gantry of seven bays, six of which have old mirrors, including one for 'Murray's Edinburgh Ales'. In the fifth bay is a door to the office behind, and on the top of the gantry are six old spirit casks. The carved bar counter is the original, and the public bar is separated from the rest of the interior by a low partition, which has lost its door. To the left, the terrazzo floor indicates changes to the layout, including losing a snug and turning two rooms into a lounge. The lounge has old panelled walls but the gantry was replaced in early 2005 and the bar counter is also modern. There is another lounge on the far left and a two-part games room at the rear served by a hatch, but all of these rooms have modern fittings.

The mirrored back gantry at the Red Lion, Kelso.

Oxton

3 Main Street TD2 6PN
01578 750235
Not Listed
Meals Fri, Sat, Sun evenings

The little-altered public bar of the Tower Hotel, Oxton.

Tower Hotel ☆

A small hotel built in 1903 in typical Edwardian style, with an angular corner tower. The public bar is still intact, retaining a simple counter and plain, four-bay gantry with large areas of mirrors and several drawers for cash and small items. Features include a vestibule entrance, stained and leaded pictorial front windows, contemporary fireplace and half-height panelling with vertical moulding. The lounge and dining room have no old fittings.

Selkirk

1 Market Place TD7 4BT
01750 20185
Category B Listed
🚌 95, X95
No food
Real ale

Town Arms

A small town centre pub with a local's stand-up public bar. In relative terms, the U-shaped bar counter is large compared to the space for customers. In order to create more room, the counter was cut back in 2006 by some 40cm (16in), although this is not obvious as the floor was replaced at the same time, and modern shelving took the place of the modest gantry. Erected in 1876 with a distinctive gabled frontage, the building became a pub in 1905. The former public meeting room, defined by an area with a cornice containing Scotch thistles, was expanded to the right by the absorption of a passage. The public bar has four large advertising mirrors: two for Drybrough's and one each for Jeffrey's IPA and Bertram's Scotch Whisky. The wall-panelling was replaced *c*.1985. A former snug at the back on the left is now a darts room. The upstairs room has modern bar fittings. Note the rare metal fly-screens (advertising Drybrough ales) in the front windows.

Tweedsmuir

on A701 ML12 6QN
01899 880272
Category C(s) Listed
Meals: Ring to check
Real ale

Crook ☆

An early 19th-century coaching inn (although claimed to date from 1580) with an extension added *c*.1936. Most of the Art Deco fittings of that era, including the finest surviving ladies and gents loos, have been retained. Walk through the terrazzo-floored lobby and past the period hotel reception to find Willie Wastle's Bar at the rear. This is just as it

The 1936 fittings in Willy Wastle's Bar of the Crook, Tweedsmuir.

was, with a 1930s lapped wood door and bar counter, gantry of shelves, stone fireplace with a circular hearth and copper hood. Even the chunky furniture – chairs, tables including a barrel one, and corner seat – is original. A visit to the toilets is a must for the vitreous wall panels (two-tone blue in the ladies; cream with black and red frames in the gents), Art Deco weighing machine in the ladies, mirrors and plumbing. As this guide was being compiled, the pub had closed and an application to convert it into a house and four flats submitted to Scottish Borders council. A campaign to reject these plans and get this remarkable inn reopened is underway so please ring for an update prior to any proposed visit.

SOUTH AYRSHIRE

Ayr
2 Castlehill Road KA7 2HT
01292 280391
Category C(s) Listed
≥ Ayr
No food

Market Inn

This late 19th-century building was saved from demolition by a local action group, which included the Ayrshire branch of CAMRA, when the surrounding area was redeveloped c.1999. A popular drinkers' pub, it still has many fittings from c.1900, and is one of a handful with an original horseshoe-shaped counter still with the old terrazzo spittoon trough around the base, which, unusually, has a drain. At the rear right where the trough finishes, the counter has been turned through 90 degrees to create more space for customers. The pub retains its original quarry-tiled floor, panelled walls that run all around the room and two Edwardian red-glazed brick fireplaces. Note the Art Nouveau stained and leaded panels in the original vestibule entrance around the right-hand door. On the left are two open snugs separated by a modern partition. The upstairs function room has an old crescent-shaped bar counter and a back gantry originally from the Marine Bar in Ayr, which was demolished in the 1990s.

81

SOUTH LANARKSHIRE

Auldhouse

12 Langlands Road G75 9DW

01355 263242

Not listed

Meals lunchtimes and early
   evenings; restaurant
   lunchtimes and evenings

Real ale

Auldhouse Arms

A 200-year-old single-storey village pub that has been enlarged in recent years but retains, little changed, its original public bar and two-sitting-room core. The public bar has a splendid quarter-circle gantry, with four upright spirit barrels, that probably dates from the 1920s. The curved bar counter, with a noticeable slope on the left side, and the floor-to-ceiling matchboard panelling are also from the 1920s, but the quarry-tiled floor is new. A tiny shop to the right was absorbed into the pub in the 1970s and is now a snug, with the pub entrance moved from the centre of the public bar to the right. The panelled rear snug has old mirrors and basic bench seating. Sadly, the front snug with its 1920s tiled fireplace was opened up by the removal of the wall in February 2006, following a customer consultation that resulted in a 58% vote in favour of the alteration. There are a number of old brewery, whisky and soft drinks mirrors. The premises to the left of the pub were purchased in the early 1990s and contain a new lounge bar, dining room and function room.

The original single-storey public bar at the Auldhouse Arms, Auldhouse remains little altered.

The tiny rear sitting room at the Auldhouse Arms, Auldhouse.

Bothwell

1–3 Main Street G71 8RD
01698 853526
Category C(s) Listed
No food

Camphill Vaults

Built *c.*1900 of red sandstone, this pub originally consisted of the public bar, family department, sitting room on the right and lounge on the left. The public bar still has its original, decoratively carved quarter-circle bar counter and a splendid, near full-height, two-sided back gantry made of rosewood. Judging by the photograph taken 70 years ago that hangs in the bar, the only change has been the removal of small spirit casks and the replacing of the clock. Part of the screen that originally separated the family department in the mid-1990s has also been removed. The high-ceilinged room has a Victorian-tiled fireplace, decorative cornice work and good ceiling roses. On the front right, the small sitting room has some old fixed seating. The narrow lounge on the left has been refurbished but there is still hatch service. There have been some additions, including a new snug behind the bar and two games rooms at the rear on the right.

At the Camphill Vaults, Bothwell, note the unusual resting place for the flap allowing staff access behind the counter. Normally it is lifted up and a catch holds it in place to allow entry but here it drops down and fits into a recess into what looks like a wooden case.

Hamilton

289 Glasgow Road,
Burnbank ML3 0QC
01698 307310
Not Listed
≢ Hamilton West
No food

Empire Bar

A basic urban pub built in 1907 in classic island bar-style. It retains its original island bar counter with short partitions and some front panels that were added in the 1980s. The dividing strips, ornamented with a badge and a diamond, are original; the Formica bar top is new, and running just underneath it all the way along is a match-striker. The original two-part island gantry has a modern top section. The old vestibule entrance on the Glenlee Street side has three doors, one of which originally led to the family department. There is a shallow vestibule on the Glasgow Road side entrance. The two open sitting rooms on the left look little altered since the 1930s; the small lounge at the rear is now a store room.

Larkhall

3–5 London Road ML0 1AQ
01698 883463
Category C(s) Listed
⇌ Larkhall
No food

The little-altered Village Tavern,
Larkhall.

Village Tavern ★

Popular drinkers' pub in a late 19th-century sandstone building, last
fitted out between the two world wars in island bar-style. The island
counter has ribbed panels except for the front section, which may
indicate the loss of a jug and bottle. The modest island gantry with
space for staff to walk through the central part has an old till drawer
that was in use up to 2000. There are wood-panelled walls to picture-
frame-height all around, fixed slatted benches, a 1920s tiled fireplace,
two old brewery mirrors, Murray's window screens and a decorative
cornice. The partitioned area in the far right corner is a spirits
cupboard, which has a '5' on the door. There were two small sitting
rooms at the rear but both are now used for storage. Some customers
still get table service on a shout of 'Hoy'.

Uddingston

60 Old Mill Road G71 7PF
01698 812678
Category B Listed
⇌ Uddingston
Meals Ring to check
Real ale

Rowan Tree

An early 19th-century, single-storey building that was remodelled in
1902–3 by architect Alexander Cullen. The pub retains its original
long bar counter in the stand-up bar, with smart sitting rooms either
side in 1970s extensions. The central vestibule entrance has three
doors with etched and frosted glass, which all now lead to the main
bar, following the removal of the centrally placed jug and bottle and its
two partition walls c.1980. The carved back gantry has impressive
mirrors hanging from the top advertising 'Wm Whitelaw & Sons India
Pale Ale' and 'James Jamieson Waverley Brewery, Edinburgh'. At each
end of the gantry there are small glazed cigar cabinets, while on the
counter are two working water taps. Other old fittings include
decorative carved Victorian fireplaces on the left and right, and a
phone box in a small screened-off area with a door and hatch.

WEST DUNBARTONSHIRE

Renton

123 Main Street G82 4NL
01389 752088
Category C(s) Listed
⇌ Renton
No food

Central Bar ★

Built in 1893, this pub occupies the ground floor of a two-storey tenement in a somewhat unprepossessing area. Behind the rather run-down frontage is an interesting interior. The unspoilt, wood-panelled public bar has a sweeping semi-circular bar counter and a very elaborate ceiling and cornices. The gantry against the side wall houses old spirit barrels in each of its four bays; unusually, every barrel has two taps and is, presumably, divided internally. There is also a free-standing gantry for bottles, glasses etc. On the left of the pub at the front is an intact jug and bottle compartment. There are old advertising mirrors, including a painted and gilded one for Old Oak Tree Whisky above the modern, rough stone fireplace. At the rear there are two sitting rooms (it seems that, originally, there were two more on the right of the pub) with floor-to-ceiling panelling, but the left one has been opened up to the bar (note the slatted seating). A new lounge is being built at the rear.

The U-shaped counter and jug and bottle compartment at the Central Bar, Renton

WEST LOTHIAN

Broxburn

7 Station Road EH52 5QF
01506 856347
Not Listed
No food

Masonic Arms

A late 1890s corner pub that consists of a long, narrow stand-up bar with a five-bay back gantry holding six spirit casks. The public bar, which is likely to have been divided in two by a partition in the past, retains its fine original bar counter. There is half-height panelling throughout, and also etched window screens, with one inscribed 'T Bain Masonic Arms', and an old 'Usher's Pale Ale' mirror. The vestibule has 'Bar' etched in the door panel. Through a large archway at the rear is a games room, which was previously two rooms.

Linlithgow

179 High Street EH49 7EN
01506 844434
Category B Listed
≋ Linlithgow
No food

Crown Arms

Early 19th-century, small town pub with a little-altered bar and a small pool room. The tiny jug bar on the left is no longer separated, following the removal of the partition *c.*1980, but the colourful window glass was retained and is now resited at the rear of the bar. Both the back gantry, with a large 'Wm Braithwaite' mirror as a centre feature, and the wood-panelled walls with benches attached could be 100 years old. The bar counter has been replaced, possibly 30-odd years ago, but it retains an old set of disused handpumps and a water tap. There are two large brewery mirrors advertising 'Bernard's Pale Ale', and one for 'John Jeffrey's Mild & Pale Ales' situated over the fireplace, and another for Mitchell Whisky. The inner doors have 'Crown' and 'Bar' on colourful glass panels. At the rear of the bar up a small flight of steps is a pool room, which has been brought into use in recent years.

West Calder

43 Main Street EH55 8DL
01506 871475
Not Listed
≋ West Calder
Meals Mon to Fri lunchtimes and
    evenings; all day Sat and Sun

Railway ★

Built *c.*1900, this little-altered, archetypical Scottish town bar with a corner turret attracts a wide range of customers. It has heavy original fittings in the form of a U-shaped bar counter, disused (but intact) jug bar with hatch as you enter, and modest island gantry (effectively in two parts with an arched walk-through central section). The dado-panelled walls are original; the large Teacher's 'Celebrated Whiskies' mirror could be 100 years old but the seating and floor covering are new. Carrying on down the passage on the right you will find a lounge at the rear, also with old dado panelling and good cornices. Visit the gents, if you can, for the mightily impressive marble urinal, tiled dado walls and quarry-tiled floor.

The splendid island gantry at the Railway, West Calder

WESTERN ISLES

Stornoway, Isle of Lewis
32 Point Street HS1 2XF
01851 701990
Not Listed
Ferry: Ullapool to Stornoway
No food

Criterion Bar

Small, single-room traditional bar in a two-storey building that remains unchanged for many years. The gantry, bar counter and fixed seating all probably date from the 1930s, and there are some good window screens. Closed on Sundays.

Heritage Pubs of the Future?

Although this guide is about genuine heritage interiors in Scotland's pubs, it would be wrong to suggest that all modern pub schemes are of no interest. Sadly, most refitting and remodelling from the mid-1960s is generally of little architectural or design interest and will probably not stand the test of time. But, thankfully, this is not true of all of them. Here is a selection of the best. Who knows, could these become the heritage pubs of the future?

The following three pubs are all faithful recreations of traditional Scottish bars carried out in the past 20 years by Ian Whyte, from what were previously run-down tenement pubs. The only genuinely old items in them are the brewery and whisky mirrors but all the materials used for the bar fittings are of the highest quality and should stand the test of time. These pubs are well worth a visit. The Bow Bar and Thompson's still use tall founts to dispense their real ales (see page 77).

Bow Bar

80 West Bow, Edinburgh EH1 2HH
0131 226 7667
Snacks lunchtimes
Real ale

Cumberland Bar

1–3 Cumberland Street, Edinburgh EH3 6RT
0131 558 3134
Meals lunchtimes; snacks all day
Real ale

Thompson's Bar

182–4 Morrison Street, Edinburgh EH3 8EB
0131 228 5700
Meals lunchtimes; snacks all day
Real ale

In the past ten or so years, we have seen banks and insurance companies abandon prestige national or regional offices, and many of them have become pubs. The following half a dozen 'new' pubs have stunning interiors, which we recommend for their architectural merit.

Archibald Simpson

5 Castle Street, Aberdeen AB11 5BQ
01224 621365
Meals all day
Real ale

A former North of Scotland Bank, now Clydesdale Bank, of 1839 by Archibald Simpson, with a quadrant Corinthian portico and a 1.8m- (6ft-) high terracotta statue of Ceres, the Roman goddess of plenty, above. The former banking hall, approached by a mosaic floor, has Corinthian pilasters, a gilt Parthenon frieze, superb ornamental plasterwork and a splendid timber and glass screen creating a separate passage on the right.

Dome

14 George Street, Edinburgh EH2 2PF
0131 624 8626
Meals all day
Real ale

Behind an imposing columned façade is a fabulous Victorian building of 1846–7 by David Rhind for

The interior of the **Dome**, Edinburgh, at Christmas when a huge tree, with lights that change colour, is perched on the new circular bar.

the Commercial Bank, the interior of which was altered by Sydney Mitchell in 1885. At the rear of the square, columned, staircase and hall lobby is the former banking hall in the style of a Graeco-Roman temple with a marble mosaic floor, arched ceilings and a mightily impressive coffered central dome. On the left, Frazer's Bar is a true replica of a 1930s Art Deco cocktail bar on an ocean-going liner, created in the mid-1990s by Ian Whyte.

Standing Order

62–6 George Street, Edinburgh EH2 2LR
0131 225 4460
Meals all day
Real ale

What was once the Edinburgh branch of the Glasgow-based Union Bank has now been colonised by Wetherspoons and forms one of their most imposing city centre outlets. The top-lit rectangular banking hall forms the main bar, and the subsidiary offices provide a series of smaller spaces. Note the mighty safe. The building dates from 1877–8.

Tiles

1 & 2 St Andrew Square, Edinburgh EH2 2BD
0131 558 1507
Meals all day
Real ale

This Early Renaissance four-storey building of 1892–5 by Alfred Waterhouse & Son was a regional headquarters building for Prudential Insurance and has its high-ceilinged former public office completely tiled from floor to ceiling in buff, brown, cream and light blue. There are two central pillars supporting lateral arches. The building has been put to good use as a pub with a centrally placed bar, and there is more tiling in the corner entrance porch.

Corinthian

191 Ingram Street, Glasgow G1 1DA
0141 552 1101
Meals all day

Built by David Hamilton in 1842 and remodelled in 1879 by John Burnett, this was the head office of the Union Bank of Scotland. It is now a super-pub with a large, square banking hall dominated by an 8m (26ft) diameter glazed dome. It is a rich blend of Renaissance decoration with representations of four continents in the cornices – Africa, Europe, the Americas and Asia – and plaster friezes. The restaurant also has a lavish interior.

Counting House

2 St Vincent Place, Glasgow G1 2DH
0141 248 9568
Meals all day
Real ale

Former Bank of Scotland office by J T Rochead, 1867–70 in Italian Renaissance style. It has been splendidly reused as a Wetherspooon's pub with a magnificent spacious former banking hall containing a glazed dome and 16 caryatids. It has a number of small rooms, and the old bank safes are still in situ.

No wonder this Victorian insurance office was renamed **Tiles** when it became a pub.

Glossary

Art Nouveau windows at the Bull, Paisley.

Air compressor/Air pressure Scotland's unique method for dispensing draught beer (see page 77).

Ale Originally fermented malt liquor made without hops. The term has been effectively interchangeable with 'beer' for at least 200 years. *See also* Real ale.

Art Deco A decorative style used in some 1930s pubs, typically featuring streamlined shapes, angular patterns and smooth surfaces.

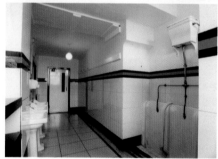

The Crook, Tweedsmuir, has the finest Art Deco loos in the UK.

Art Nouveau A decorative style used in some *c.*1900 pubs, typically featuring flowing, sinuous forms, often of stylised flowers. Charles Rennie Mackintosh, Glasgow's famous architect, was one of the leading practitioners of Art Nouveau.

Arts and Crafts An artistic movement *c.*1900, affecting all the decorative arts as well as architecture, that stressed high-quality craftsmanship (ideally hand-made rather than machine work), fine surface textures and beauty of design.

Beer Alcoholic drink made from malted barley, hops and water, plus yeast to promote fermentation. *See also* Real ale.

Bell Box A small box with a series of windows which is visible to bar staff (see page 12). When a customer presses a bell for table service a disc or flap moves to show which sitting room or snug is in need of attention.

Bell-push The device to summon a waiter and obtain table service (see page 12).

Caryatid A sculptured female figure, usually of plaster, in the form of a support or pillar.

Cask beer/Cask-conditioned ale *See* Real ale.

Family bar/Family department *See* Jug and bottle.

Formica A laminated material developed in the 1930s in the USA and introduced into Europe in 1946. It became popular for covering bar tops in the late 1950s due to its easy-to-clean properties.

Fount A dispenser on a bar counter from which draught beer is served (see page 77).

Gantry, back and island The (often very ornamental) shelving, cupboards, etc. at the rear or in the centre of the servery (*see* Servery) used to house bottles,

The back gantry at the Grill, Aberdeen.

glasses, measures, etc. and occasionally casks. This fitting is known by its own Scottish name 'gantry', derived from 'gantress', or 'gauntress', old words to describe a wooden stand for barrels (see the sections entitled Island serving counters and Ornate gantry with spirit casks on pages 6–9 of the Introduction).

Island bar A style of pub design, introduced mainly in Scottish towns and cities in the 1890s and early 1900s, consisting of one large, open-plan room with, usually, an oval-shaped serving counter in the centre (see the section entitled Island serving counters on page 6–7 of the Introduction).

The island bar counter at the Pittodrie Bar, Aberdeen.

Jug and bottle/Jug bar A small room in a pub where drink can be bought for consumption off the premises. It is usually accessed through a separate door and screened off from the rest of the pub (see Family Department on page 10 of the Introduction).

Ladies' room/Ladies' snug A small room in a pub set aside for use by women and usually accessed from its own front door (see page 9 of the Introduction).

Pot-shelf Superstructure standing on a bar counter to hold (usually) glasses. Most of these have been added in the last 30 years.

Real (or traditional or cask-conditioned) ale All beer is brewed with malted barley, hops and water, plus yeast to promote fermentation. With real ale, fermentation is in two stages. The primary fermentation takes place at the brewery. Then the beer is put in casks and sent to pubs, where a secondary fermentation takes place. The cask has to be left undisturbed so that sediment can sink to the bottom. Real ale is best served at a cellar temperature of 11 to 12°C. With keg and smooth beers, the fermentation is killed off in the brewery by pasteurisation, and the product is served under artificial carbon dioxide, or a mixture of carbon dioxide and nitrogen pressure, at temperatures as low as 4°C to mask the bland or, at times, unappetising flavour.

Servery The area from which drinks are served, typically including the counter, gantry and the space in between.

Sitting room A room of varied size with plenty of seating in contrast to the main stand-up bar (see page 9 in the Introduction).

Snug A very small sitting room.

Spirit cocks Pubs often held bulk stocks of sprits, usually on upper floors, and these were dispensed through taps (= cocks) on the gantry. Only six sets are still known to exist in the UK, one of which is at the Bull, Paisley.

Spittoon trough Situated around the base of a bar counter originally to collect spit, sawdust, cigarette ends and other detritus. They were still being installed as recently as the 1950s and 60s, but many have now been removed or covered over.

Tenement Scotland's dominant style of urban house building with the ground floor often occupied by a shop/shops or a public house with a block of flats above (see page 5 in the Introduction).

Terrazzo Small pieces of marble set into a fairly soft cement or mortar, rubbed down and then polished. Popular in pubs as a hard-wearing material for floors, toilets and other heavy-use surfaces.

Traditional ale *See* Real ale.

Veneer A facing of a thin sheet of fine wood disguising a coarser, cheaper underlay.

Water engine Part of a once-common system for serving draught beer in Scotland (see page 77).

Window screen A small window panel placed at eye level and often containing a brewery or whisky advertisement. Some can be made of metal and are then called 'fly screens'.

A window/fly screen at the Town Arms, Selkirk.

Public Transport to the Pubs

This guide indicates where pubs are close to a railway station or, in Glasgow, a subway station. For Aberdeen, Dundee, Edinburgh and Glasgow pubs, we show the number of bus services, where they run every 10 or 15 minutes during the day from Monday to Saturday (those in brackets run every 20 minutes or more). In addition, there are many local bus services, so it is possible to reach the majority of the pubs in this guide without driving.

A great way to get around Scotland by public transport is with a Freedom of Scotland Travelpass. You can buy the 'any 4 out of 8 consecutive days' ticket for £100, or the 'any 8 out of 15 consecutive days' ticket for £135 and there is a 33% discount for Senior Citizen and Young Person Railcard holders. These tickets give unlimited rail travel within Scotland after 9.15am on weekdays and all weekend, and are also valid on all Caledonian MacBrayne scheduled ferry services within Scotland. There is also a Central Scotland Rover ticket for any 3 out of 7 days unlimited rail travel costing £30. Full details and conditions can be obtained from FirstScotrail on 08457 550033 or www.firstscotrail.com

Bargain Travel around Edinburgh
Lothian Buses have an excellent value Day Saver Ticket at £2.30 that you can buy on the bus at any time of day. For their services after midnight you will need a separate, all-night travel ticket costing £2. Lothian buses require the exact fare. For more information, ring 0131 555 6363 or visit www.lothianbuses.co.uk.
First Bus have a number of routes from the city centre to outlying areas and a FirstDay ticket costs £2.30. More information can be found at www.firstgroup.com

Bargain Travel around the Glasgow Area
Strathclyde Passenger Transport (SPT) has a Discovery Ticket with unlimited travel for one day on the subway for £1.90, available from any underground station; a Roundabout Ticket offering unlimited travel for one day by rail and subway in the Glasgow and Lanarkshire area for £4.50 and a Daytripper Ticket offering one day's unlimited travel by rail and subway, that includes most buses and some ferries throughout the former Strathclyde region (i.e. East Ayrshire, East Dunbartonshire, Glasgow, Inverclyde, North Ayrshire, Renfrewshire, South Ayrshire, South Lanarkshire, West Dunbartonshire and part of Argyll & Bute). This costs £8.50 for 1 adult and up to 2 children (5 to 15 years inc.). All these tickets, which are available from manned railway stations and SPT Travel Centres, can be used after 9.30am during the week and all day at weekends. For more information, ring SPT on 0141 333 3708 or visit www.spt.co.uk

The largest operator of buses in the Glasgow area is First Bus, which offers a FirstDay Ticket costing £2.85 before 9.30am and £2.55 thereafter. For more information, ring 0141 636 3124 or visit www.firstgroup.com

Timetable and Ticket Information
Buses: For details on how to reach towns and villages by bus throughout Scotland, contact Traveline on 0870 6082608 (if calling from outside Scotland press 6 as soon as you hear the recorded message), or visit their website, www.traveline.co.uk. Alternatively, visit the new UK complete journey plan website www.transportdirect.info

Coaches: Scottish City Link run long-distance coach services in Scotland (08705 505050 or www.citylink.co.uk)

Trains: For information on services throughout Scotland, contact National Rail Enquiries on 08457 484950 or visit www.nationalrail.co.uk.

Ferries: Caledonian MacBrayne operate many ferries to Scotland's islands and have good-value Island Rover and Island Hopscotch tickets. Contact them on 08705 650000 or at www.calmac.co.uk

Please note that all ticket prices quoted are as of January 2007 and are subject to change.

Index